AWS

A Comprehensive Guide to Mastering Amazon Web Services

Aaron Hudson

Table of Contents

What is Cloud Computing?

Almost all IT solutions carry the term "cloud computing" or cloud solution. Such buzzwords can help sales, but they are difficult to use in a book. So, for clarity, let's define some terms.

Cloud computing is a metaphor for the provision and consumption of computer resources. Cloud computing resources are not directly visible to the user; There are layers of abstraction between the two. The level of abstraction offered by the cloud varies, from offering virtual machines (VMs) to providing software as a service (SaaS) based on complex distributed systems. Resources are available on request in large quantities and you pay for what you use.

Cloud computing refers to the two applications provided as Internet services and the hardware and software systems of the data centers that provide these services. Data center hardware and software is what we call a cloud. Cloud computing is a quite a new concept and has recently become popular. The cloud takes advantage of virtualization technology and, in the essence of cloud computing, there is a logical separation between the different nodes, each node appears as a different physical machine for the user. Unlike grid computing, many distributed computers are connected to one another to form a large logical computer that can handle large amounts of data and calculations. In the case of cloud computing, virtualization technology makes each node appear as a separate physical machine, allowing the user to load custom software and operating system at each node and configure custom rules for each node.

The idea of cloud computing comes from parallel transformations, ordered distribution and grid computing. There is some similarity between them, but they work otherwise. Although cloud computing is an emerging field of competition, the idea has been around for years. This is called cloud computing because data and applications exist in a "cloud" of web servers. To simplify the concept, cloud competition can only be defined as sharing and using applications and resources in a network environment to work without worrying about ownership and management of network resources and applications. According to Scale, with cloud computing, the IT resources needed to get the job done and your data are no longer stored on a personal computer, but instead are stored elsewhere so that they are accessible anywhere, anytime.

and start a geophysical modeling application available everywhere. This could include the ability to rent a virtual server, load software on, enable or disable at will, or clone to respond to a sudden workload load. These can include warehousing and securing large amounts of data accessible only to authorized users and applications. It can be compatible with a cloud provider that configures a platform that can automatically adapt to work changes. This may involve using a storage cloud to store applications, businesses and personal data. And this may be the ability to use a lot of web services to embed photos, maps and GPS information to create a page in customers' web browsers.

In a cloud computing system, the workload is drastically altered. Local computers no longer need to run applications. The cloud computing network manages instead. In this situation, the demand for hardware and software from the user is reduced. Let the cloud handle. The only thing local computers need to know is the interface software running the application. Today, a web browser like Mozilla Firefox and Internet Explorer 8 is widely used as interface software in a cloud compatibility system. The truth is that Internet users have already used some form of cloud computing. If you have an email account with a web-based email service, such as Hotmail, Yahoo! Mail or Gmail, I had some experience in cloud computing. Instead of running an email program on a local computer, the user remotely connects to a webmail account. Software and account storage does not exist on the local computer, but in the cloud services.

Three distinct features distinguish cloud computing from traditional hosting. First, it is sold on demand per minute or hour. Secondly, it is elastic. A user may enjoy all or part of the services requested at any time. Third, the service is managed entirely by the provider. Significant improvements in virtualization and distributed computing, as well as improved access to broadband Internet, have increased interest in cloud computing.

Cloud computing has changed the way we create and deploy applications. With Amazon Web Service's cloud marketing platform, we can exchange custom hardware and infrastructure with virtual servers and easily configure storage, security and network services. Just pay for the computing power you need. Learn some strategies and techniques and you can be sure that your applications will be running in AWS in minutes.

Public, private, and hybrid clouds

Basically, there are three types of cloud in cloud computing: public, private and hybrid cloud. In a public cloud, external service providers make resources and services available to their customers over the Internet. Customers' applications and data are implemented in an infrastructure owned and trusted by the service provider. A private cloud offers many of the same benefits as a public cloud, but the services and data are managed by the organization or by a third party, solely for the organization of the client. In general, private spaces in the cloud increase the administrative costs of the client, but enable better control of the infrastructure and reduce security concerns. The infrastructure can be located inside or outside the organization's structures.

A hybrid cloud is a combination of a private cloud and a public cloud. The decision on what works between the private cloud and the public cloud is usually based on a number of factors, including the commercial importance of the application, the sensitivity of the data, the required certifications and industry standards, regulations, etc. However, in some cases, the peaks of resource demand are still managed in the public cloud.

Cloud computing is generally characterized by providing three types of functions, namely IaaS, PaaS and SaaS, where aaS is a shortcut for "as a service" and the service implies that the function is not local to the user but the place. in a remote location accessible via a network). The letters I, P and S in acronyms refer to different types of functionality, as the following list clearly shows:

Infrastructure as a Service (Iaas): Provides users with the basic concepts of computing: transformation, network connectivity and storage. (Of course, you also need other features to fully support IaaS features, such as user accounts, usage tracking, and security). You need to use an IaaS cloud provider if you want to create an application from scratch and need access to low-level functionality in the operating system.

Platform as a Service (PaaS): Instead of offering low-level features in the operating system, it provides high-level programming frameworks with which a developer interacts to get IT services. For example, instead of opening a file and writing a collection of bits in it, in a PaaS environment, the developer simply calls a function and then provides the collection of bits. The PaaS structure handles tedious work, such as opening the file, writing in bits, and ensuring that the file system has received the bits. The PaaS infrastructure provider is responsible for backing up data and collecting backups, for example, to prevent the user from doing other tedious administrative tasks.

Software as a Service (SaaS): It has evolved to an even higher level in the evolution of PaaS. With SaaS, all the features of the application are sent over a network in one package. The user only needs to use the application; The SaaS provider addresses issues related to the creation and operation of the application, the separation of user data, the security of each user, as well as the whole SaaS environment and the treatment of a large number of others. details.

As with all models, this division in I, P and S provides an explanatory influence and seeks to make cleanliness and cleanliness an element that, in real life, can be quite complicated. In the case of IPS, the model is presented as if the types were defined correctly, though. Many cloud providers offer many types of services. Amazon, in particular, has begun to provide a variety of platform-based services as its offerings develop and even venture into full-featured application services offered in partnership with SaaS. You can say that Amazon provides all three types of cloud computing.

Private versus cloud computing

If you find that the combination of I, P and S in the previous section is confusing, expect that you will hear about the distinction between public and private cloud. Consider the sequence of events:

1. Amazon, as the leading cloud computing provider, offers public cloud computing: anyone can use it.

2. When considering this new creation of Amazon Web Services, many IT companies were asked why they could not create and offer an AWS-like service to their own users, hosted in their data centers. This on-premise version is known as private cloud computing.

3. Continuing the trend, many hosting providers think that they can offer their IT customers a separate part of their data centers and allow customers to create clouds there. This concept can also be considered private cloud computing because it is dedicated to a user. On the other hand, since data from and from this private cloud is running on a shared network, is the cloud really private?

4. Finally, after discovering that companies could only choose the public or private sector, the term hybrid was coined to refer to companies using both public and private cloud environments.

As you move through the cloud, you will probably see a lot of discussion about which of these cloud environments is best. My personal position is that regardless of when you are in the private / public / hybrid problem, public cloud computing will undoubtedly become an important part of each company's IT environment. In addition, Amazon will undoubtedly be the largest provider of public cloud communication. It makes sense to plan for a future that includes AWS.

Key function of cloud computing

There is no standard definition or specification for cloud combination. Defining the key features of Cloud Computing based on field practices can take some time. Based on practices in the service design and solution design sectors, the following two key triggers could play a key role in this innovative phase of cloud computing:

Virtual technology

Virtualization technology is used to manage how the operating system, middleware, and image of the application are processed and mapped to a physical machine or part of the server stack. Virtualization technology can also help reuse licenses for operating systems, middleware, or software applications when a subscriber releases their service from the cloud communication platform.

Service Oriented Architecture (SOA).

A service-oriented architecture is essentially a suite of services. These services communicate. Communication may involve a simple transfer of data or two or more services coordinating an activity. Some ways to connect the services are required. The evolution of a programming system or architecture is now approaching services, unlike many decades, most applications are standalone and unique.

Recently, the giant growth of the Internet user and the availability of Internet technology, the use of software can now be curbed. Giant companies like Google, Microsoft, Sun or even Amazon can have this ability to provide software services instead of selling the software directly to the user. SOA is a software or system architecture that addresses component, reuse, scalability and flexibility. All of these features are a fundamental need of companies looking to save on choices instead of buying.

Why People Choose Cloud Computing over Dedicated Server:

Its Advantages

Each client has its own inclination be it with how every individual uses the figuring technology or amplify the possibilities of the Internet technology. The way people see the utilization of technology relies upon what kind of requirements they have and how every technology can assist them with settling their needs. Presently, contingent upon how every individual sees the ease of use of that technology, its advantage turns into a variable.

Numerous people who utilize the Internet and its highlights see the cloud processing as the technology that bears many advantage contrasted with its known "rival, the devoted server. The following are a portion of the features that make cloud registering more favored than the other.

a. Cloud processing is known to be entirely versatile. With cloud processing what you by and large need is a PC that is associated in an Internet and you can productively drive results. Not at all like with a committed server, you should always carry alongside you your framework since every one of the records that you need are on a server.

b. Cloud registering isn't constrained to a solitary resource. With cloud figuring, you are not constrained to utilizing what your devoted server can give you. With the huge resources of Internet, you are given such huge numbers of decisions where to draw your resources.

c. Cloud processing has better security over the committed servers. The Internet all alone has an exceptionally solid and dependable security. Despite the fact that the issue about being defenseless is there, security has been firmly watched with all conceivable potential assaults.

Have you recently acquired budgets for managed data centers and virtual computing? If you are used to getting quotes from web services from your service provider, the steps described here can help you request quotes for managed services. First, most cloud data centers and services display package pricing on their websites. You can see the costs or costs defined for storage, data transfer and data requests.

You will usually receive a fixed monthly rate for these services. However, there are web service providers and data centers that charge users for each use. It is up to you to decide which range of services will suit your needs. If you are a great user and plan to use a lot of storage and bandwidth, it is better to contact the customer service department directly. You can get a favorable contract from these companies. Second, there are data centers and web service providers with online citation capabilities. Use this function to request a specific budget for data transfer purposes. This service is usually provided free of charge so you can buy the best prices available with confidence.

Once you've received your budget, you can also contact your provider's sales department to see if you can get a better price. Getting a quote for data center management services is easy today. Due to strong competition, some companies will allow you to negotiate a better price for the service.

The Amazon Business Philosophy

Amazon Web Services was officially unveiled to the world on March 13, 2006. On that day, AWS offered Simple Storage Service its first service. (As you can imagine, Simple Storage Services were quick to point to S3.) The idea for S3 was simple: it could offer the concept of object storage on the Web, a configuration in which anyone could place an object, essentially any group of bytes. . - in S3. These bytes can include a digital photo, a backup of a file, a software package, a video or audio recording, a spreadsheet, or the idea that suits you. S3 was relatively limited to its beginnings. Objects can be written or read from anywhere, but can only be stored in one region: the United States. In addition, the objects cannot exceed 5 GB, which is by no means smaller, but certainly smaller than many files that users may want to save in S3. The actions available to objects were also quite limited: I could write them, read them and delete them, and it was so.

In its first six years, S3 has grown in all its dimensions. The service is now offered worldwide in different regions. Objects can now reach up to 5 terabytes. S3 can also offer many more functions with respect to objects. An object may now have an end date, for example: you can set a date and time after which an object is no longer available for access. (This feature can be useful if you want a video to be available for viewing only for a certain period of time, for example, the next two weeks). S3 can now also be used to host websites. In other words, individual pages can be viewed as follows. Objects and their domain name (www.example.com, for example) refer to S3, which serves pages. S3 is not the only example of AWS. Only a few months after launch, Amazon began offering the Simple Queue Service (SQS), which allows the transmission of messages between various programs. SQS can accept or send messages in or out of the AWS environment to other programs (such as your web browser) and can be used to create highly scalable distributed applications.

Later in 2006, Cloud Elute Computed (affectionately known as EC2). As an AWS IT service, EC2 offers on-demand competition capabilities with immediate availability and no uptime commitment. So, from a single service (S3) to over 25 in just over six years and worldwide, they are constantly growing and improving! He is probably impressed by how quickly it all happened. You are not alone In the industry, Amazon is viewed with a mixture of fear and envy because of the speed with which it offers new AWS features.

The AWS commercial application includes:

Alexa for business

Alexa for Business is a service that allows organizations and employees to use Alexa to do more work. With Alexa for Business, employees can use Alexa as a smart assistant to be more productive in meeting rooms, at their desks and even with Alexa devices that are already at home.

Amazon WorkDocs

Amazon WorkDocs is a fully managed and secure enterprise service and engagement service with administrative controls and feedback features that improve user productivity. Users can comment on files, send to other users, and download new versions without having to e-mail multiple versions of their files as attachments. Users can enjoy these features wherever they are, using the device of their choice, which includes PCs, Macs, tablets and phones. Amazon WorkDocs offers IT administrators the ability to integrate with existing corporate directories, flexible exchange strategies and control over where the data is located.

saved You can start using Amazon WorkDocs with a free 30-day trial that provides 1 TB of storage per user up to 50 users.

Amazon WorkMail

Amazon WorkMail is a secure, managed and professional messaging calendar and service that supports existing mobile and desktop email client applications. Amazon WorkMail offers users the ability to easily access their emails, contacts and calendars using the client application of their choice, including Microsoft Outlook, iOS and Android native messaging applications, any the client compatible with the IMAP protocol or directly. Through a web browser. You can integrate Amazon WorkMail into your existing corporate directory, use the email body to meet compliance requirements and control the keys that encrypt your data and the place where they are stored. You can also configure interoperability with Microsoft Exchange Server and programmatically manage users, groups, and resources with the Amazon WorkMail SDK.

Amazon Carillon

Amazon Chime is known as a communication service that transforms online meetings with a secure, easy-to-use and reliable application. Amazon Chime works perfectly on all your devices so you can stay connected. You can utilize Amazon Chime for online meetings, video conferences, calls, discussions and to share content, inside and outside your organization. Amazon Chime works with Alexa for Business, which means you can use

Alexa to kickstart your meetings with your voice. Alexa can start your video meetings in large conference rooms and automatically participate in online meetings in smaller meeting rooms and in your office.

The Infrastructure of AWS

If Amazon is doing AWS is a revolution, as described in the previous section, how is the company doing? In other words, how do you provide this wonderful service? Throughout this book, it describes in detail the operation of the service, but for now describes the general approach taken by Amazon to build AWS. First, Amazon approached the business in a unique way, as did a company that changed the face of the sales company. Amazon specializes in a low-margin business approach and integrates this perspective into AWS. Unlike almost all other players in the cloud marketing market, Amazon has focused on creating a highly efficient, low-margin offering. This offer starts with the way Amazon has built its infrastructure.

Hardware Decisions

Unlike most of its competitors, Amazon builds its hardware infrastructure from standard components. In this case, the term "good" refers to the use of equipment by lesser-known manufacturers who charge lower prices than their competitors. For components because there is no product offering available, Amazon (known as a proud merchant) offers extremely low prices. From the hardware side of the AWS offering, Amazon's approach is clear: buy the cheapest hardware possible. But wait, you say the product-based approach doesn't provide a less reliable infrastructure? After all, branded hardware vendors claim that one of the benefits of paying higher prices is that you get a better computer. Butter. . Yes and no. It can be certain that first-class equipment (traditionally called business equipment because of the assumption that larger companies need more reliability and are willing to pay more for it) is more reliable when comparing apples to honey. That is, a corporate server will last longer and experience fewer failures than its product-class counterpart.

From Amazon's point of view, the issue is how much hardware hardware is more reliable than the consumer version and what value has this improved reliability. In other words, it is necessary to know the cost / benefit ratio of the company compared to the basic product. Adjusting this rating is a fundamental fact: on the Amazon business scale (remember that it has nearly half a million servers running its AWS service), the computer, regardless of its provider - is below. If you are a cloud vendor with an Amazon-sized infrastructure, you have to assume, for each type of hardware you use, a number of hard drives, motherboards, network switches, delete packages, and so on.

Therefore, even if you buy the most expensive, highest quality hardware, you will always find yourself (if you have the opportunity to become a very large cloud computing provider like Amazon, for example) with a small infrastructure. reliable. In other words, on a large scale, even extremely reliable individual components always result in unreliable general infrastructure for component failures, as rare as a failure in a specific piece of equipment can be. The scale of Amazon's business also affects other aspects of its hardware infrastructure. In addition to components such as servers, networks, and storage, the data centers also have power supplies, refreshers, generators, and backup batteries. Depending on the specific component, Amazon may need to use properly designed equipment to operate at the required scale.

Think of the AWS hardware infrastructure this way: If you have to design and operate large data centers and align with the mandate of a company to operate at a lower cost, you will probably get a very similar solution. to that of Amazon. You will use the basic hardware as much as possible, the lowest prices when you cannot get basic products and hardware designed to handle your exceptionally large operations.

Examining Amazon's Software Infrastructure Strategy

Because of Amazon's broad demands, you probably expect it to take a unique approach to the cloud software infrastructure that runs in your hardware environment, right? Be aware that Amazon has created a unique and highly specialized software environment to offer its services in the cloud. I emphasize the word because, at first glance, people often find AWS to be different and confusing: there seems to be no other computing environment they have encountered before. Once users understand how AWS works, they generally find that their design makes sense and is appropriate for the quality of their services and, most importantly, how users use the service.

Even though Amazon takes an unusual approach to its hardware environment, it is in the software infrastructure that its uniqueness really stands out. It allows you to give a quick description of its features. The software infrastructure is:

Based on virtualization: Virtualization, a technology that destroys software components beyond the underlying hardware dependency, is the core of AWS. Being able to create virtual machines, start, finish and upgrade quickly enables AWS service.

As expected, Amazon has approached virtualization in a unique way. Of course, I wanted to use virtualization economically, which is why I chose the Xen Open Source hypervisor as the basis for the software. Subsequently, he made significant changes to Xen's "vanilla" product to meet AWS requirements. The result is that Amazon uses virtualization, but the proposed virtualization solution is expanding to support large scale and offer endless services.

Operated as a service: I know you are saying, "Of course, it works as a service, that's why it's called Amazon Web Services!" That is true, but Amazon had to create an extraordinary software infrastructure to be able to offer its computing capabilities as a service. For example, Amazon needed to create a way for users to leverage their AWS resources remotely and without requiring local interaction. And I had to separate a user's resources from other user's resources to ensure security, because no one wanted other users to see, access or modify their resources.

Created for flexibility: Amazon has designed AWS to target multiple users - users who need sophisticated IT services available at all times to meet the needs of their applications and constantly changing work conditions. In other words, like Amazon, you can't predict what your IT needs will be in a year or two, or the market for which

Amazon has created AWS. In this situation, it makes sense to implement few restrictions on the service. Therefore, instead of offering a set of strictly integrated services that provides only a few ways to use it, Amazon provides an extremely granular set of services that the user can "combine and combine" to create an application that exactly matches their needs. . by designing the service in a very flexible way, Amazon allows its customers to be creative, thus promoting innovation.

High resistance: If you consider that hardware content is unreliable, you will now find that there is no way to implement resistance through hardware. The obvious alternative is to use software, and this is the path chosen by Amazon. Amazon makes AWS highly resilient by deploying resource redundancy, essentially using multiple copies of a resource to ensure that failure of a single resource does not cause service. For example, if you store a single copy of each of your objects in your S3 service, this object may sometimes become unavailable because the disk drive where you resided has failed. Instead, AWS retains many copies of an object, which guarantees that even one or two. - Objects are not available due to hardware failure, users can also access the object, improving the reliability and durability of S3.

Counting Up the Network Effects Benefit

The reason why the AWS ecosystem has become the IT market for everyone can be understood in the network effect of the phrases, which can be considered as the value derived from a network because other network participants are part of to stay. network. The classic case of the network effect is the phone: the more people use a phone, the more valuable the phone is. In fact, the larger the number of phones used, the easier it is to communicate with a large number of phones. And on the contrary, if you're the only person in town who has a phone, well, you'll be pretty alone, and not very talkative! In other words, for a service with network effects, the more users there are, the more attractive it is to potential users and the more value they will receive when using the service.

From an AWS perspective, network effect means that if you provide a new cloud-based service, it's a good idea to offer them where there are many other cloud users, such as AWS. This network effect greatly benefits AWS, simply because many people, when they start thinking about using cloud computing, naturally match AWS because it is a brand they recognize. However, for AWS, the network effect is even more important than the fact that many people use it: the technical aspects of AWS also play an important role. When one service communicates with another over the Internet, communication between Internet services takes a while. Even at the speed of light, information that travels long distances is time consuming. Additionally, while information is circulating on the Internet, it is constantly redirected to routers to ensure it is sent to the correct address. This combination of network length and device interaction is called latency, a measure of the delay imposed by the distance of network traffic.

Specifically, if you use a web browser to access data from a website hosted 50 miles from you, it will probably respond faster than if the same site was hosted 7,000 miles. To continue with this concept, using a nearby service speeds up the execution of your application, which is always a good thing. Therefore, if your service runs on AWS, you want all the services that depend on it also runs AWS, because the latency of your application is much less than if these services were created elsewhere.

People who create services tend to be smart, so note that their potential customers like the idea of having services nearby. If you create a new service, AWS will attract because many other services are already located. And if you plan to use a cloud service, you will probably choose AWS because the number of services offered will facilitate the creation of your application, from the point of view of service availability and low latency performance. The network effects associated with AWS provide you with a wide range of services to use when building applications to run on Amazon's cloud offering. They can help you reduce your workload and accelerate the development of your applications by moving away from the traditional burden of integrating software components and external services into your application.

Here are some of the benefits of using AWS ecosystem network effects in your application network:

- The service is already operational in AWS. You do not need to get the software, install it, configure it, test it and integrate it into your application. As it is already operational in the AWS environment, you can go directly to the last step: perform the technical integration.
- Services have a cloud-compatible license model. Providers have already figured out how to deliver their software and billing in the AWS environment. Providers often align with the AWS billing method, billing at the time of use, or offer a monthly access subscription. However, it is worth using a provider that charges high license fees and negotiates to operate in the AWS environment; This is already done.

- Support is available for service. You must not understand why a component of the software you want to use does not work well in the AWS environment: the provider assumes responsibility. In the slang of the support world, you have, as the tech industry says quite clearly, throat-slapping.

- Performance improves. Because the service works in the same environment as your application, it provides low latency and helps your application work better.

Before you start thinking about finding a built-in software application to integrate with the application or writing your own software component to provide certain features, search the Marketplace to see if one or more applications already have the features you need.

AWS versus Other Cloud Providers

Nature hates emptiness and markets hate monopoly suppliers. Otherwise, competitors are always entering an attractive market. Cloud ordering is no different: there are many cloud providers. It is, of course, you want to know the AWS performance level. The biggest difference between AWS and almost any other cloud provider is the target market. To understand this aspect, you must understand the basis of the service offered. Now, AWS is born from features developed by Amazon to allow its developers to quickly build and deploy applications. The service aims to make developers more productive and, in a word, happier. On the other hand, most other cloud providers have a legacy of hosting: their background includes support infrastructure for IT operations teams to maintain system availability. The high quality of their infrastructure traditionally forms an important part of the value proposition of hosting providers, that is, the commercial nature of their servers, networks, warehouses, etc. This legacy has several implications for business cloud providers:

- The focus is on IT operations concerns rather than developers. It is often reflected in the following message: "The service is not easy to use." For example, a business cloud provider may need to have a discussion with a representative before giving access to the agent. service, then imposes a manual process as part of the account configuration. Instead, AWS allows anyone with an email address and credit card to access the service in ten minutes.

- The service itself reflects its hosting heritage, with its features and usage model that reflect the functioning of the physical servers. Often, the only storage offered by an enterprise cloud service provider is associated with individual virtual machines. Object storage, such as S3, is not offered because it is not part of a typical guest environment.

- Cloud service providers often require a multi-year commitment to utilize resources with a specific level of IT capability. While this strategy facilitates cloud service provisioning to plan your business, it is far less convenient for users, and imposes some of the issues they are trying to escape from!

- The use of commercial equipment often involves higher prices compared to AWS. I have already seen that cloud service providers charge 800% more than AWS. Depending on the needs of the organization and the nature of the application, users may be willing to pay more for these providers. On the other hand, higher prices and long-term commitment that often accompanies the use of an AWS competitor may seem unattractive or unacceptable to many users.

Benefiting from Web Services

Since other aspects of our lives go online (banking, shopping, tax payments, joining, socializing), people naturally want to be able to combine two or more into a new one. Creation This is the technological equivalent of the musical mash-up that I am currently writing: a combination of two elements to create a new one that reflects the parts of both. One of the first examples of this phenomenon is an Internet application that combines Google Maps with craigslist apartment listings to create a map that identifies the location of each available apartment. The only application was to combine (mix) two basic services, but from this union comes an extremely useful result: an apartment guide in a particular area, which makes the process of selecting some to show and get a much more effective route. . The huge growth of mobile computing, the new world of smartphones and tablets, has fueled the growth of APIs and mashup applications. The "application culture" of mobile computing is a natural place to combine services, especially those related to location. Applying the apartment plan just described is even more useful when it is accessible to the flight. Are you finished looking for an apartment? Open the app and let me show you where the closest apartment is for rent.

The next big frontier for web services is the so-called "Internet of Things," a term that refers to computer devices not used by humans, but between them, that interact to do useful work (appliances). smart ones that communicate with utility company billing). systems, for example). Soon, though, you'll be surrounded by all kinds of devices that constantly interact with cloud-based applications. What will be the size of the Internet of Things? A senior Cisco official predicts that 1 billion devices will interact online soon. There is growing evidence (if necessary) that the world today is a world of web services, businesses, government agencies and non-profit organizations putting their resources in API-accessible online form. Engineers combine online web services to create new applications that combine individual services and provide unique and useful features.

- This web services revolution I describe has several interesting benefits:
- Innovation: Web services promote innovation and music mixes allow people to combine music resources with new creations. While you may not be

able to perceive the value of a combination of, for example, fuel consumption indicators, local fuel prices and national park reviews, another may conclude that "A request from a person enters the Model and Your car model for getting to know the parks you can visit for less than $ 25 in gas costs would be fairly correct, and many people might agree. (Actually, I can put this app on my to-do list !)

- Niche market support: In a world of non-web services, the only people who can develop applications are those who work for organizations. I am the only one who has access to computer resources or data. The only applications developed are those that the company finds useful. However, once these resources and data are available via web services, someone can create an application that allows applications to be developed for niche markets. For example, a person can combine Google Maps with a city bus schedule in a mobile application to allow users to see when and where the next nearby bus will be available.

- New sources of revenue: Companies can provide a web service interface to their business transaction systems and allow outside entities to sell their products. For example, the large Sears retailer has enabled mobile application developers and bloggers to sell Sears products through a Sears web service.

These developers and bloggers are reaching out to the audience that Sears cannot reach, but Sears can succeed without being involved. As another example, Netflix has made its web services interface available for video offerings, and many device and game manufacturers have used it to integrate Netflix with their products. Netflix can earn new revenue every time someone buys a Wii or Xbox and decides it would be great to use their new game to access movies and TV online.

AWS Components

AWS offers a variety of infrastructure services. The AWS service list is a growing list of services, many of which are in preview mode at some point. In this section, we will discuss some of the major AWS services.

Amazon Elastic Cloud Computing (EC2)

Amazon EC2 is a web service that provides AWS capable cloud computing. You can group the operating system, application software, and related configuration settings into one Amazon Machine Image (AMI). Then, you can use these AMIs to provide multiple virtualized and dismantled instances with so-called web services. EC2 instances can be resized and their number increases or decreases depending on your needs or your demand. These instances can be started in one or more geographical locations or regions and in availability zones. Each region has multiple availability zones located in separate locations, connected by low-latency networks in the same region. Amazon Elastic Block Storage (Amazon EBS) volumes provide persistent network-connected storage in EC2 instances. Elastic IP addresses allow you to assign a static IP address and programmatically assign it to an instance. You can enable monitoring in EC2 instances with Amazon CloudWatch. You can create automatic resize groups using the automatic resize feature to automatically resize their capabilities based on CloudWatch metrics. You can also distribute incoming traffic using the Elast Load Balancer (ELB) service. You can also use the AWS CloudTrail service to monitor the AWS API and AWS SDK calls for your account. Amazon EC2 Container Service is a cluster management and configuration service. This service allows you to start and slow down applications that use a container through the API.

Amazon S3

Amazon S3 is a highly durable and distributed data warehouse. Through a web service interface, you can store and retrieve large amounts of data as objects in compartments (containers). The stored objects are also accessible from the Web via HTTP.

Amazon EBS

Amazon EBSs are persistent, highly available, and persistent block-level storage volumes for use with Amazon EC2. Configure EBS with SSD (general purpose or IOPS arranged) or magnetic volumes. Each volume of EBS is automatically replicated in its availability zone.

Amazon CloudFront

Amazon CloudFront service is a CDN service for distributing low latency content (static or streaming content). For example, copies of S3 objects can be distributed and cached in many peripheral locations around the world, creating a distribution network using the Amazon CloudFront service.

Amazon Glacier

Amazon Glacier is a low-cost storage service that is generally used for archiving and backup. Data recovery time in Glacier can be up to several hours. Other AWS storage services include the Amazon Storage Gateway (allows integration between the local environment and the AWS storage infrastructure) and the AWS import / export service (which uses portable storage devices to allow large amounts of file transfers data in and out of the AWS environment). .

Amazon RDS

The Amazon Relational Database Service (Amazon RDS) provides an easy way to configure, use, and develop a relational database in the cloud. Available AWS database options include MySQL, Oracle, SQL Server, PostgreSQL, and Amazon Aurora (preview below). You can start a database instance and access a complete MySQL database, while reducing the workloads associated with common database administration functions such as backups, patch management and more.

Amazon DynamoDB

Amazon DynamoDB is a NoSQL database service offered by AWS. It supports document / key-value pairs, data models and has a flexible layout. Integration with other AWS services, such as Amazon Elastic MapReduce (Amazon EMR) and Redshift, supports Big Data and BI applications, respectively. In addition, integration with AWS Data Pipeline provides an efficient way to transfer data to DynamoDB.

Amazon ElastiCache

If your application requires intensive reading, you can use the AWS ElastiCache service to drastically improve the performance of your applications. ElastiCache also supports Redis cache and memory solutions. AWS ElastiCache supports increased reliability to automatically detect and replace failed nodes, automates patch management and allows monitoring for integration with Amazon CloudWatch. ElastiCache can be scaled according to the application load.

Simple Amazon glue service

Amazon Simple Queue Service (SQS) is a distributed, reliable, highly scalable, hosted, and distributed queue that stores messages as they move between computers and application components.

Simple Amazon notification service

Amazon Simple Notification Service (Amazon SNS) provides a simple way to notify applications or people from the cloud application. Use the publish / subscribe protocol.

Virtual Private Cloud Amazon

Amazon Virtual Cloud Cloud (Amazon VPC) allows you to expand your corporate network into a private cloud contained in AWS. Amazon VPC uses the IPSec tunnel mode which allows you to create a secure connection between a door in your data center and a door in AWS.

Route 53 of Amazon

Amazon Route 53 is known as a highly scalable DNS service that allows you to manage your DNS records by creating a hosted area for each domain you want to manage.

AWS Identity and Access Management

AWS Identity and Access Management (IAM) allows you to control access to AWS services and resources. You can create users and groups with unique security credentials and manage permissions for each of these users. You can also define IAM roles so that your application can securely call APIs without creating or distributing your AWS credentials. IAM is natively integrated with AWS services.

Amazon CloudWatch

CloudWatch is a monitoring service for your AWS resources. It allows you to retrieve monitoring data, set alarms, troubleshoot problems and take action based on problems found in your cloud environment.

Other AWS services

There are several other AWS services that help you manage your cloud environment. These include CloudTrail (record AWS API calls), AWS Config (provides you with an inventory of resources and current configuration of your AWS resources), AWS CloudHSM (helps you meet contractual obligations and / or compliance) and AWS Key Management (to be managed). your data encryption keys).

In addition, AWS provides several services to implement and manage your applications. These include AWS

Elastic Beanstalk (to deploy web application scales), AWS OpsWorks (an application management service), AWS CloudFormation (to provide a set of associated AWS resources) and AWS CodeDeploy (to automate code implementations).

AWS services associated with other applications include Amazon EMR (an infrastructure hosted by Hadoop), Amazon Kinesis (to ingest and transmit data), Amazon SWF (a workflow service), Amazon AppStream (for cloud streaming), Amazon Elastic Transcoder (to convert media files), Amazon SES (a bulk messaging service) and Amazon CloudSearch (for applications that need scalable search service functionality). AWS also offers payment and billing services that will benefit from Amazon's payment infrastructure. In addition to the services provided by Amazon, many software products and services are offered by external suppliers through the Amazon Marketplace. Depending on the needs of your app, you can choose to integrate these services into your applications instead of creating them.

It is conceivable to host a full website on Amazon S3 yet Amazon evangelists will urge you to utilize another server to host your full site. Amazon S3 is principally a data storage service. Server side registering and preparing of contents isn't secured by S3 services. These procedures ought to be performed by the server of your web hosting supplier. Be that as it may, Amazon S3 services can be valuable and practical in the event that you use it to host your media files. Move of media files, for example, pictures, recordings, music, and huge documents, can hinder the server of your web site. This implies more slow downloads and uploads. Service interruption can likewise occur if these media files are dealt with by your web host.

That is the reason you will require a data storage solution like the Amazon S3 to host huge files. Simply divert the traffic for download or upload request to your Amazon S3 site. This viably appropriates your data transfer capacity so you can maintain a strategic distance from moderate execution and service downtimes. Download and upload requests can be taken care of productively by Amazon S3 services. Actually, there are numerous photograph sharing and long range informal communication sites that are utilizing Amazon S3 data storage service. These websites host their media files on Amazon to unburden their servers. You can likewise utilize Amazon S3 to back up your web files and documents. These archived documents will consume significant disk space on your web hosting server. So as to convey your archived files, just host it on Amazon and recover them at whatever point you need.

Common Myths About
Amazon Web Storage.

Stories about not controlling uncontrolled cost data, there are so many myths about cloud computing and AWS. Whether you are a cloud-based professional or a cloud-based company, you want to be able to distinguish myths from realities.

Let's look at other common myths about Amazon Web Services.

Myth 1: The cloud will cost me a fortune

Have you calculated your installation costs on the site? Don't forget to add losses due to the inability to deal with high traffic or the cost of maintaining a massive infrastructure when your site is not occupied. When using the cloud, you can avoid unnecessary expenses and pay for resources only. actually using them AWS applies a billing template as it progresses. As your business grows, you will pay for additional computing resources still available. On the other hand, next month, if your business is a bit slow and consumes less resources, your bill will be lower. This type of system saves you the huge upfront costs and serious investment you need to build your own infrastructure. . It also indicate that there are no additional costs than those that come with the services you actually use. By comparing these two numbers, you have to realize that you are saving money by using the cloud and that it does not cost you a fortune.

Myth 2: I can only utilize the cloud for storage

This is not true. Yes, there are cloud storage providers like Box, Dropbox, Microsoft Onedrive or Google Drive, but today we are not talking about such services. We talk about IaaS (infrastructure as a service) cloud systems from providers like AWS, Microsoft Azure and Google Cloud. You can use it for all kinds of activities. For example, thousands of business, government, educational and other organizations use Amazon's web services to host their websites, create various types of applications, run and analyze big data, organize research. IT projects and performs all types of activities, including information storage. Cloud computing is much more than just data storage, and it's good to know you can enjoy the benefits of such a system at any time.

Myth 3: Control my data less with the cloud

It is commonly accepted that cloud servers control the service provider and that there is not much to do. Its control is reduced to a basic configuration while the "higher power" does all the rest. But that's not how things work. With a cloud configuration, completely control your data in real time. Using simple monitoring mechanisms, you can find everything you need to know about your instances. For example, you can see who launched the instance, where, from when it was running, and the applications running in that instance and the data used.

Myth 4: Data transfer to the cloud is all or nothing

No, you do not need to migrate all your data simultaneously to the cloud. It would be wise! Instead, every sensitive and massive migration of activities to the cloud needs to be carefully planned and executed in several stages. All you need to do is set the right pace for your team and let them do the work. If you need help along the way, you can:

- Use many resources available online
- Get help from an AWS Support Center
- Find a local AWS partner company to help you migrate.

Myth 5: Everyone can access my data in the cloud

This myth could be replaced as: "Who knows who else has access to my data in the cloud?" The fear of data intrusion and espionage is inevitable. This is one of the biggest obstacles when considering using a cloud infrastructure. However, such claims and fears are not useless. Do you think Netflix, NASA, Capital One and Airbnb would be willing to put their business at risk if anyone could access their data stored on AWS? When your data is stored in the cloud, you have the absolute power to decide who can access your settings. You are the one who determines who will have access, even the level of authorization. Technicians working as AWS network administrators do not have access to their instances. Even when they solve problems, their access is quite limited. Knowing this, you can be sure that you are the only leader in your cloud universe.

Myth 6: I did not control the location of my data.

Again, this is not true. There is only one leader as far as your cloud configuration is concerned. It also means you have complete control over where your data goes. AWS has server centers around the world. You can choose the data center that you will use during the initial configuration. If you decide to use a data center in Ireland, your data will be stored wherever you are. Nothing else can do.

Myth 7: It is very difficult to teach my team how to use AWS.

Introducing new technologies into a computer is not always easy, but it is certainly not impossible. Just like any other news, the acceptance of cloud technology may not be immediate. But like any new technology, there will certainly be some fans and first-time users on your team who will advocate and support change. There are many resources available to help your team adopt a new technology. You can use many resources to learn more about AWS (and even get some very useful certificates at the same time as the method), you can use:

- AWS learning materials
- Online training platforms, such as Cloud Academy, offer training for both individuals and complete teams.
- Follow online discussions and best practices.
- Get help from your local AWS partner

Myth 8: My on-premise setup is more secure than the cloud

Are you sure that your setup has a higher level of security than the cloud? Think again. Safety is a top priority of AWS and other cloud vendors that are doing their best to make sure that the data on their servers stay secure and safe from any illegal cyber activities.IaaS infrastructure is designed to be "bulletproof" and resistant to common web security issues such as SQL injections, XSS, CSRF, etc. An army Engineers strive to improve the security of their data stored in the cloud every day. They all create a flexible, automated and secure computing environment that you can use. Now, compare a complete and carefully constructed system that is precisely tuned for over 10 years from your local configuration. Even if you have the best and most talented team, it is highly likely that they will not be considered for the latest security updates or that you are missing something that may cause a problem sooner or later.

Myth 9: Cloud services do not have all the certification I need for my business.

Another common mistake is that cloud services do not have certification capabilities and are inaccessible to businesses that require specific standards and certificates. You would be surprised to know that most of them are certified to an even higher level of your needs. You can utilize AWS Certificate Manager and get the certificate that is required for your business. You can use this service to meet compliance needs, minimize the inability of your services, and improve the ranking of your searches. In addition to the standard SSL / TSL certificates, you may need specific certificates. For example, AWS has a program for government institutions and also meets the FBI standard for Criminal Justice Information Services (CJI). It is helpful to know if you work with compression agencies and if you have clients who need compliance.

Myth 10: AWS is only for big companies

AWS is a highly scalable system. It can support large and demanding systems such as Amazon.com, Netflix or banking systems. It can also be used for small businesses and start-ups. Did you know that AWS has a startup program called AWS Activate? With this program, your small business will be able to manage the services when needed and, even if it's small, your costs will be minimal. Some of the largest startups in the world have used AWS Activate to grow. Did you know that Slack, Airbnb and Pinterest started on AWS? You can also start here and grow your business from scratch, as they did.

Reasons to Use Amzazon Web Service

AWS provides IT agility

It is known as the "non-department". Admittedly, some computer organizations seem to enjoy stubbornness similar to that of Dilbert, where innumerable and inexplicable obstacles prevent anyone from accessing the magic of "infrastructure," others feel frustrated by the complexity. organize many different resources, each with its own interfaces and configuration rules, all of which must be successfully combined to provide access to computer resources. Most of these manual, tedious, and multi-compartmental efforts are the result of long-established, mass-produced processes, leading to IT performance cycles that typically require weeks or months for resources to be available. team. As a result, everything is slower than molasses and widely despised. Amazon, as usual, has reshaped the approval process as if it were built from scratch and implemented as an integrated, automated service. Because every part of the infrastructure is managed by an API, human interaction is not required for the installation or configuration of resources. And, since services are downstream (IP addresses are managed separately from storage, for example), resources can be defined and started in parallel instead of having to do it step by step.

AWS provides business agility

Guess which one? If you are a business unit in a company (sales or human resources, for example), you are what you call IT "without a department". And facing a slow moving IT organization today is not only embarrassing, it is also dangerous for your business. This danger stems from the changing nature of computer applications. In the past, IT applications mainly automated the company's internal processes (payment, billing, document management) commonly known as registration systems because they were registered information. Apps are now much more likely to be used to interact with customers or, in fact, "to meet their needs." These applications are often called commitment systems because they promote engagement with parties outside the organization. And the rise of smartphones, tablets and sophisticated sites is raising the level of customer expectations.

In other words, to satisfy current customers, companies need to quickly deploy new applications, to be agile, in other words. And AWS offers great business agility. It's no secret that an important part of the AWS user base consists of business entities that adopt AWS as a way to bypass the IT process and their extended provisioning processes. This adoption of business unity is sometimes referred to as ghost or, even more, pejorative and dishonest computing. Regardless of the name you call, this adoption is made because business units feel the need to quickly deploy new applications to meet market demands, and AWS helps organizations speed up their response time to be more agile.

AWS offers a rich ecosystem of services

Another disadvantage for other cloud service providers is the work that users have to do to create applications that use functions such as queue, administrative alerts, dynamic scaling in response to the cloud load. the user, etc. Although these other services provide on-demand virtual machines, building applications with software components and external services is left up to the student's performance, so to speak.

As a result, creating an application can take a long time because the developer needs to install and configure the software components, which takes time. For components that require a business license, you must arrange payment, which can be time-consuming, given the complexities of budget approval and contract negotiation. Online services (for example, a tax calculation service) may not be available from the chosen cloud service provider, which requires an internet call to access the service elsewhere online, which requires a network latency and adversely affects application performance.

Amazon makes application development faster and less challenging with a rich ecosystem of services that can deliver the benefits of your favorite search engine:

▪ A range of services as part of your AWS offering: These services range from basic items, such as object and volume storage, to platform services, such as files and emails. to complete applications, such as Elastic MapReduce. and Redshift.

- Services hosted on AWS by several external companies: for example, Informatica and Dell Boomi offer application integration services on AWS. AWS users can integrate applications into AWS through these services, and network traffic should never leave AWS, which reduces network latency and improves application performance.

- All locally developed AWS services (and most third parties) are offered with the same pricing model as AWS: prices are standardized with simplified contracts that can be executed online. The result is that users can avoid long-term contract negotiations and large prepayments in favor of on-demand payments, which corresponds to the AWS user.

The rich AWS ecosystem is one of the least known but most valuable aspects of AWS. Speed of response (agility, in other words) is crucial today for businesses in general and IT in particular. The rich AWS ecosystem promotes agility and is an important reason for using AWS.

AWS simplifies IT operations

IT operations are a daunting task, and will never end. In fact, the term Sisyphus may have been coined to describe the eternal work of managing computer resources. First, because AWS is responsible for most of the traditional IT infrastructure (buildings, power, networks, and physical servers, for example), a lot of work is underpinned by IT tasks and the burden of operations. Computer science is on the decline. right away.

By simplifying IT operations, AWS allows its users to focus on the really important part of IT: applications. In fact, AWS allows a user to spend more of their IT budget on features that differentiate their business, while allowing them to reduce their investment in important but non-differentiated operations associated with "keeping the lights on."

AWS Enables Innovation

Wherever you go, the word innovation is a hot topic. People recognize that innovation improves lives and can improve the future of future generations. Given my enthusiasm for AWS, it's probably not surprising that I truly believe that cloud computing doesn't exist without Amazon's presence. The major players in the existing technology market are not encouraged to change their working methods. It takes a foreigner like Amazon, who had no protection, to rethink how technology is provided. AWS has changed the way it delivers technology to customers and, as a result, led to a burst of news.

The innovation and low costs associated with AWS allow small and large companies to launch new offers quickly and profitably. As one innovation consultant explained, "AWS has reduced the cost of failures. AWS allows you to easily test a new product to see if it is," he added. "Also, if a new offer takes hold and starts to accelerate, AWS allows it to expand easily. However, if the service fails adoption, it is not a problem: the ease of closing AWS resources means that nothing is lost. if a possible innovative offer does not materialize. "

AWS is good for your career

A good career is about being the right person in the right place at the right time. Being the right person depends on you: your ability to work hard, your productive working relationships, and your intelligence, for example. These features will help you to succeed regardless of the field or position in which you work. It can be in the right place at the right time: it has a lot to do with the vision of a new market, possible from a kind of innovation, emerging and planting its flag. People who started in the automotive industry in the 1920s or the television industry in the 1950s or the Internet in the 1990s have been facing huge opportunities since a new market has sought knowledge. It is necessary to create large companies. Technological innovation creates huge gaps in the skills of the industry and makes people with knowledge and experience invaluable. If you believe AWS is the next generation of platform, it may still be the "right place at the right time" for you.

Getting Started with
Amazon Web Service

Never fear that Amazon offers its own web user interface to work with AWS. This interface, the AWS management console, hides all the complex details of interacting with the AWS API. Interact with the console and the Amazon program addresses all the complexities under the hood. In fact, many people never interact with AWS, except for the console: it's also powerful. This chapter introduces you to the console, explains how to set up your AWS account, and also gives you an overview of cloud computing. You can interact with the AWS S3 storage service, upload a photo of your choice and connect to the Internet and view it in your browser. How fun

Amazon updates console screens quite frequently. As a result, the screenshots in this manual may be different from what you see on your device. Fortunately, it is generally very easy to assign the features of one version of the screen to another, but I wanted to preview it before I was afraid to see a screen that differs from that of the book. Changes in the management console view are a side effect of rapid change and innovation in AWS.

Setting Up Your Amazon Web Services Account

The first thing to do is to create your AWS account. In this multi-step process, you register the service, provide your billing information and then confirm your agreement with AWS to create your account. Coming soon? Let's go directly to:

1. Point your favorite web browser to the Amazon Web Services homepage at http://aws.amazon.com.

2. Click the Register button.

On the next screen, you can log in with an existing AWS account or install a new account. Create new account.

Technically, you can also use your current Amazon sales account, if any, even if I don't recommend it. Think about it. If you split up your AWS account and used a marketing ID, someone with whom you have your AWS might end up buying a nice big flat screen TV. I recommend setting up a new AWS account.

3. Make sure the radio button is selected I am a new user, type the corresponding email address in the field provided and click on Connect to our secure server button.

AWS will take you to a new page where you will be asked to enter your login information.

4. Enter a username, your email address (twice, to be sure) and the password you want to use (again, twice, just to be safe).

5. Click the Continue button. This opens the Information Account screen and asks for your address and phone number. You will be asked to check the box to confirm that you accept the terms of the AWS Client Agreement.

6. Enter the required personal information, confirm the acceptance of the customer agreement and click on the Create account button and continue. The next page will ask for a credit card number and your billing address. Amazon needs to make sure you get paid, right?

7. Enter the required payment information in the corresponding fields and click Next.

The next page you see is a little curious. Amazon wants to confirm your identity and therefore asks for a phone number to call you.

8. Enter your phone number in the appropriate field and click call now. AWS displays a PIN on the screen and then calls the phone number you provided.

9. Answer the phone and enter the PIN indicated on the keypad of the phone.

10. Click on the Continue button. It requires you to wait a bit for AWS to set up your account, but in my experience, it doesn't take more than two or three minutes. You will then receive an email confirming your account settings. You must click on a link in this email to complete the account registration process.

Once the configuration is complete, you will see a screen that lists all the services for which you are already registered automatically, just to create your account. A pretty impressive list, right?

Here are two important points to take away from this initial account setup:

- Your account is now set up as a general AWS account. You can use AWS resources anywhere on the AWS system: the eastern United States or one of the two zones in the western United States, Asia Pacific (Tokyo, Singapore or the United States). Australia), South America (Brazil) and Europe (Ireland). In other words, your account covers all the AWS, but the resources are in a specific region.

- You have provided AWS with a credit card number to pay for the resources you use. In fact, it has an open tab with AWS. Be careful about the amount of computing resources you consume. For the purposes of this book, you do not have to worry about costs, since your initial registration provides a level of service for one year which should be sufficient to meet the stages described in this book, as well as to conduct experiments without you. break your savior

If you're corncerned about spending too much on AWS, Amazon will support you. You can set up a billing alert with an amount you don't want to exceed. If your total use of AWS for a month approaches this figure, Amazon will send you an alert. You can enable invoice alerts by clicking on My Account on the Admin Console homepage and then clicking on Account Activity on the next page. That's right. Everything is already installed on AWS and ready to start cloud computing. If you are a bit like me, you are eager to do some testing just to see how AWS works. Get ready to do a little operation with AWS: Stock up and find a photo of the AWS Object Storage Service called S3.

Access your first AWS service

After you are the proud owner of an AWS account, it's time to do something useful. Start checking your S3 resources. To do this, click on the S3 link on the home page of the AWS admin console. You will have access to a page that allows you to manage your S3 resources. If you have piercing eyes, you will immediately notice that there is nothing on the page. The first thing to do is to create a storage resource where you can place your first object. However, before I explain step by step the process of creating a storage resource, I want to talk a bit about terminology. You will see a button called Create compartments to the left of the S3 screen. Now you can ask that something that appears to be purchased in a store is prominently featured on AWS. The answer is simple: AWS refers to all higher-level identifiers in S3 as cubes, which means, can mean, a place to keep things for storage. (The term "cube" may be your first exposure to the curious AWS nomenclature, but rest assured it won't be the last!)

The first thing to do is create a cube. Before you run out, consider some AWS requirements:

- Deposit names are unique throughout the AWS system. Names must be unique to all user accounts. So, if I have a pet named Star and decided to call one of my Star cubes in his honor, and another has already named one of his Star cubes, well I'm not lucky. It's not very practical, but it is.

- Even though the names of the deposits are global (in other words, unique throughout the AWS system), the deposits are located in a particular region. Suppose you want a deposit to reflect the name of your company, for example, Corpname. If you use Corpname to create a warehouse, you will isolate that name in a single region, even if you want to place objects from around the world in a warehouse associated with your business name. Therefore, a better strategy is to use a common identifier with region-specific information in the name of the deposit; For example, you can use Corpname-US-Este for a deposit in the eastern region of the United States. UU. Corpname-US-West-Oregon for a deposit in the region associated with Oregon.

- Use all lowercase letters to create a cube. Although the official S3 naming rules allow you to use uppercase letters, the S3 Admin Console does not allow you to create deposits in most AWS regions. If you try to include capital letters in the repository name, the console returns an error message. Remember, even though AWS is a great service, it has its peculiarities. You can always find a way to avoid it, but don't be surprised when you find problems that don't work exactly as AWS says.

Create your first cube

1. On the S3 home page, click the Create Deposit button. This opens a screen.

2. Enter a name for your deposit in the Deposit Name field. As this is just an experience, feel free to choose the name of your choice, without worrying, if it is a compartment name that is already in use, AWS informs you.

3. Select a region from the Region drop-down menu. Choose the article "Oregon".

4. Click the Create button. AWS creates your new account and returns to page S3 to manage your resources. You see a screen that now lists the repository you just created.

Congratulations You have now completed your first cloud treatment. Of course, it's not even useful: your cube is there, like a blank card, so put something in there to see how everything fits.

Loading data into S3 compartments

Suggest that for your first S3 experience, upload an image that you can then retrieve and view in your browser. Start on page S3 to manage your resources. Find the cube you just created. Found good!

1. Click to select the deposit you created. This opens the compartment and the right side of the screen lists a series of actions that you can perform on the cube.

2. Click on the Download button. The Upload-Select Files dialog box appears.

3. Click the Add files button.

4. Using the file selector widget that appears, browse to your local file system, select a file to download and click

Open at the bottom of the widget. Return to the Upload-Select Files dialog.

5. Click the Start Start download button in the lower corner of the dialog box. After a few centuries, your repository will list the file you just downloaded. If you click on the Properties button in the upper right corner, you will see information about the file.

Downloading the file represents half the work. Now, all you have to do, through a browser, is to access the photo you just downloaded. However, before you can do this, you must set permissions on the object to be available on the Internet to someone other than the owner (by the way, this is for you). To do this, follow these steps:

1. In the list of downloaded files, select the file you just downloaded.

2. Click on the Properties button in the upper right corner of the screen. This opens a panel that contains all kinds of information about the selected object. You can also access information about the properties of a file by right-clicking on the selected file and selecting Properties from the menu that you see.

3. Click the arrow next to Permissions.

The Permissions section expands to view permission information. You should not only look near the Recipient as someone who can access the file. You must add an authorization for others to access the file as well.

4. Click the Add Permissions link.

An additional drop-down menu (also called a Recipient) appears below the first menu.

5. Select All in this second drop-down menu, select the corresponding Open / Download check box, and then click Save.

The file is now accessible to everyone. To access it, simply search for the URL you want to use.

6. Return to the Properties screen.

Here you see an information panel about the object, including its URL.

7. Copy the URL contained in the Link section, create a new tab in your browser, enter the URL you just copied into the address line and press Enter. You have to see your image appear in the browser, just like magic!

AWS Dashboard Gives Comprehensive Web Service Status

The Amazon Web Services website was created to offer up-to-date status to Amazon users and clients. The AWS State occasionally (sometimes even every minute) releases information that has something to do with Amazon's online accessibility services. Customers and customers can access the AWS dashboard by visiting Amazon Web Services as often as they need. Details of the current state of web services can be viewed via an RSS feed if your customers and users want to be notified of changes, developments or, at times, interruptions.

The AWS board works in real time. In addition, all reports, problems, and queries related to specific web services can be transmitted through the AWS panel. For each web service presented in the table (visible in the AWS panel), there is a link that directs the user or client so that the problem or incident report can be resolved immediately. The AWS board is large and easy to move. When the website opens, you will be entitled to see a table containing the active status of the web services, including details. The details of the table inform the viewer if the web service in question is functioning normally, is having performance problems, or is interrupted.

For each detailed status, there is an informational message to inform the user / client about the actual status of the problem. Status history is also present on the AWS panel. This is because AWS wants to keep a track record or report, as well as reports and interruptions in services, to better address the problem that may occur. The table contains a history of 35 days. Therefore, if you click on a particular web service, the status history is displayed for 35 days. Customers and customers using the AWS dashboard are not alienated from what happens to every web service they use.

Delving Deeper into AWS Benefits

AWS storage

You should consider AWS Storage search for several reasons:

• Storage is an increasingly important problem for computing due to the recent and dramatic increase in the amount of data that companies use in their daily businesses. Even though traditional structured data (the database) is growing fairly quickly, the use of digital media (video) by businesses is exploding. IT companies use more and more storage and often use communications service providers (CSPs) such as Amazon to provide storage. The recent increase in Big Data, which refers to the analysis of very large data sets, is another factor in storage consumption. Companies are drowning in the data and many are struggling to manage their own on-site storage system.

• Storage is Amazon's first AWS offering. Therefore, storage is an important part of the AWS ecosystem, which includes highly innovative uses of its storage services by AWS customers over the years.

- Various AWS offerings depend on AWS storage, including Simple Storage Service (S3). Understanding AWS storage services helps you better understand how AWS offers depend on AWS storage.
- AWS continues to innovate and provide new storage services. Glacier, for example, brings yet another solution to a historical computing problem: archival archives.

This chapter will cover the four AWS storage services:

- Simple storage service (S3): Provides highly scalable object storage in the form of unstructured bit collections.
- Elastic Block Storage (EBS): Provides highly available and reliable volumes of data that can connect to a virtual machine, extract and connect to another virtual machine.
- Glacier: a data storage solution; Provides extremely robust and inexpensive file data storage and retrieval
- DynamoDB: storage of key values; provide highly scalable, high-performance storage based on tables indexed by data values called keys

You might wonder why Amazon offers four different AWS storage services. This interesting question, which is at the heart of Amazon's unique cloud computing offering, aims to respond well to the flood of data.

• Scalability: Traditional methods simply cannot scale enough to handle the amount of data that companies now generate. The amount of data that companies need to manage exceeds the capacity of almost any storage solution.

• Fast: They cannot move data fast enough to meet the demands of enterprise storage solutions. To be honest, most business networks can't handle the level of traffic needed to skip all the pieces stored by businesses.

• Cost: Given the volume of data processed, established solutions are not economically viable, are not accessible to the size that businesses now need.

For these reasons, the storage problem is passed along to the local storage (for example, the hard disk on the server using the data). Over the past two decades, two other forms of traditional storage have entered the market: network storage (NAS) and network storage (SAN), which drag storage from the local server to the network where it is installed. . When the server requests data, instead of searching for a local disk, it searches for it on the network.

The two types of network storage are very different (despite the similarity of their acronym). The NAS, which functions as an extension of the server's local file system, is used as a local file: reads and writes work the same way as if the file were on the server. In other words, NAS gives the impression that it is part of the local server. SAN works very differently. Provides separate remote storage from the local server; This storage does not appear as local on the server. Instead, the server must use a special protocol to communicate with the SAN device. You can say that the SAN device provides separate storage that the server will need special arrangements to use. Both types of storage are still widely used, but much larger volumes of data do not allow NAS or SAN storage to support the requirements. As a result, new types of storage with improved features have emerged.

In particular, there are now two new types of storage available:

> Purpose: Reliably saves and retrieves unstructured digital objects
> Key value: manages structured data

In warehouses objects

Object storage is used to store objects, which are essentially digital bit collections. These pieces can represent a digital photo, an MRI scanner, a structured document such as an XML or video file of your cousin's embarrassing attempt at skateboarding in the steps of the public library (the one she presented at her wedding). Object storage provides reliable (and highly scalable) bit collection storage, but does not require any bit structure. The structure is selected by the user, who must know, for example, whether an object is a photo (which can be modified) or an MRI scan (which requires a special application to view it). The user must know both the format and methods of manipulation of the object. The object storage service simply provides reliable storage of parts.

Object storage is different from file storage, which you can get to know better on a computer. File storage provides an upgrade function, different from object storage. For example, suppose you store the log log of a program. The program constantly adds new registry entries when events occur. create a new one

Using it every time an additional recording record is created would be incredibly annoying. On the other hand, the use of storage allows you to update the file permanently by adding new information. In other words, update the file when the program creates new records. Object storage does not offer updating. You can insert or retrieve an object, but you cannot change it.

Instead, update the object in the local application and insert it into the object store. To save the new version the same name as the previous one, delete the original object before inserting the new object of the same name. The difference may seem minor, but it requires different approaches to managing the objects looked at.

Key-value distribution storage

Distributed key-value storage, unlike object storage, provides structured storage that is somewhat similar to a database, but significantly differs in providing additional scalability and performance. You can already use a relational database management system, a storage product commonly known as RDBMS. Your data lines have one or more keys (hence the key-value storage name) that support data manipulation. While RDBMS systems are incredibly useful, they are generally facing scale problems beyond a single server.

New, key-value distributed storage products are designed from scratch to support large amounts of data across multiple servers (perhaps thousands). Key-value storage systems often use redundancy in hardware resources to avoid interruptions; This concept is important when using thousands of servers because they may experience hardware failures. Without redundancy, the entire storage system can be closed by a single server. The use of redundancy makes the key value system always available and, most importantly, your data is always available because it is protected from hardware failures. Dozens of key storage products are available. Many of them have been developed by leading web-based companies, such as Facebook and LinkedIn, to allow them to handle a considerable amount of traffic. These companies have reviewed and published the products under Open Source licenses. You (or someone else) can now use it in other environments.

Although key-value storage systems vary in different ways, they have the following common characteristics:

- The data is structured with a unique key used to identify the registry in which all the remaining data resides. The password is almost always unique, such as a username, a unique username (for example, title_1795456) or a part number. This ensures that each disk has a unique key, which facilitates scale and performance.
- Recovery is limited to the value of the key. For example, to search all records with a common address (where the address is not the key), each record must be examined.
- Searching for multiple data sets with common data elements is not supported. RDBMS systems allow for combinations: for a given username in a data set, search all records in a second data set with the

username in individual records. For example, to find all user-retrieved books from the library, join the user table (where the user name is used to identify their library ID) and the payment table (where each book is listed with the user name). the library ID of all those who have checked). You can use the combination function of an RDBMS system to

ask this question; On the other hand, since key-value systems do not support combinations, the two tables must be mapped to the application level rather than the storage systems. Using this concept, commonly referred to as "application-based intelligence", union execution requires application "intelligence" and many additional codings.

Key-value storage represents a trade-off between usability and scalability, and trading is scalability and less usability.

This proliferation of storage types gives users a much richer set of options for managing the data associated with their applications. Although they gain a lot of flexibility and can adapt the storage solution to functional requirements, they also have a challenge: a broader set of skills is needed to manage more storage solutions. In addition, using a key-value solution requires hundreds or even thousands of servers. Fortunately, Amazon recognizes that all of these storage solutions are important despite the management challenges involved, and offers four types of storage solutions. A user can choose the one that best suits his needs, without having to integrate in his application a solution that is not compatible with the necessary features. The need for storage flexibility explains why Amazon offers four types of storage. You may not need all four, many users only manage one or two. You need to understand all the AWS options it offers, so you can choose a new one instead of relying on the existing solution.

S3 storage basics

S3 objects are treated as web objects, that is, they are accessible to Internet protocols using a URL identifier.

- Each S3 object has a unique URL, in the following format: http://s3.amazonaws.com/bucket/key
- An S3 object that uses this format is similar: http: //s3-us-west-1.amazonaws.com/aws4dummies/Cat+Photo.JPG

Now, you may ask, what are the cubes and the key, given in the first example? A repository in AWS is a group of objects. The name of the tax is associated with an account. For example, the deposit called aws4dummies is associated with my aws4dummies account. The name of the compartment should not be the same as the name of the account; It can be something. However, the repository name is completely flat: each repository name must be unique among all AWS users. If you try to create a test bay name in your account, you will receive an error message because you can bet that your last earnings have been reached. (For your information, an account is limited to 100 compartments).

A key in AWS is the name of an object and serves as an identifier for locating the data associated with the key. In AWS, a key can be an object name (as in Cat + Photo.JPG) or a more complex layout that requires a structure for organizing objects in a cube (such as in the cube / photos / catphotos / Cat + Photo). JPG, where / photos / catphotos is part of the object name). This convenient layout provides a family directory type or URL format for object names; However, it does not represent the true structure of the S3 storage system. It's simply a convenient and memorable method of calling objects, which allows users to easily track them. Although many tools present S3 storage as if they were in a familiar mapping organization (including the AWS management console), they do not mean how objects are stored in S3.

S3 Object Management

An S3 object is not a complex creature, it is just a byte collection. The service does not impose restrictions on the format of the object, it is up to you. The only limitation refers to the size of the object: an S3 object is limited to 5 TB (this is great).

Objective management in S3

Like all AWS offerings, S3 can be accessed through a programming interface or API, and is compatible with the SOAP and REST interface. (For more information on the details of these interfaces, you probably should not use the (not particularly easy to use) API to publish (create), obtain (retrieve), or delete S3 objects. Through a programming library which encapsulates API calls and provides higher-level, easier-to-use S3 functions, but probably uses a higher-level tool or application that provides a graphical interface for managing S3 objects, however, make sure that somewhere in the Depth There is a call to the S3 API from the library or top-level tool.

The most obvious and useful actions for objects (such as publishing, fetching, and deleting), S3 provides a wide range of object management actions, for example, an API call to obtain the version number of an object.

I mentioned that the object does not allow an object to be updated (as opposed to a file that resides in a file system). S3 solves this problem by allowing you to control the version of S3 objects: you can modify version 2 of an S3 object, for example, and save the modified version as version 3. This avoids the process of updating objects. described above: retrieve the old object, edit the object in the application, remove the old object from S3 and finally insert the modified object with the name of the original object.

S3 bucket and object security

AWS provides detailed access controls to implement S3 security: you can use these controls to explicitly control who can do what works with S3 objects. The mechanism by which this access control is applied is, of course, the list of access controls (ACLs).

These four types of people can access S3 objects:

- Owner: The person who created the object. You can also read or delete the object.
- Specific users or groups: Private users or user groups in AWS. (Access may be limited to other members of the owner's company).
- Authenticated users: People who have AWS accounts and have successfully authenticated.
- Everyone: Everyone on the Internet (what I look like).

S3 provides a complete set of actions in the S3 API. Various functions, for example, allow manipulation of object versions to retrieve a certain version of an object. And of course, I mention elsewhere that the expiration capacity that was added in early 2012, is also in the API. Access controls specify what and what actions specify what: who can do what with a given object. The interaction between S3 access controls and object actions gives S3 better functionality for object management.

Use S3, big and small

Making specific recommendations on what to do with S3 is difficult because it is extremely flexible and capable. Individual (rather than commercial) users tend to use S3 as secure storage of digital media, regardless of their location. Another common personal use of S3 is to save local files through the AWS management console or one of several consumer backup services. Companies use S3 for the same reasons as people and for many other use cases. For example, companies look at the content files used by their partners in S3. Most electronic and device manufacturers now offer their digital user manuals; Many of them keep these files in S3.

Many companies place images and videos used on their corporate websites in S3, which alleviates storage management problems and ensures that, under heavy traffic conditions, the performance of the website is not hindered. due to insufficient network bandwidth. The most common S3 actions are:

of course, around the creation, retrieval and disposal of objects. Here is the common life cycle of an S3 object: create the object for use; set permissions to control access to the object; Allow applications and users to retrieve the object as part of an application's functionality. and remove the object when the application using it no longer needs it. Of course, many objects are never dropped because they are persistent: they have a constant purpose for a long time.

As you are familiar with S3, you will probably start exploring new features in S3. S3 offers encryption of objects stored in the service, protecting your data from anyone trying to access them inappropriately. You can record requests made to S3 objects to check when objects are accessed and what they are doing. S3 can also be used to host static websites: they do not dynamically collect data to create the pages that served as part of the website, which eliminates the need to run a web server. Many online computer services that you use (or use) as part of your personal or professional life use S3; It is increasingly used in solutions offered by large and small technology companies. The workbook on the Internet, in fact!

Purpose and availability S3

The S3 function and its use to access objects is just a piece of the puzzle. We must also take into account the general organization of S3. AWS is generally organized into regions, each of which contains one or more availability zones, or AZs. Although S3 locates deposits in regions, remember that the names of S3 deposits are unique in all S3 regions, even though the deposits are resident in particular regions. For example, if you create a deposit with your company name, you must choose the region where it is placed.

In the example of the cat photo: http://s3-us-west-1.amazonaws.com/aws4dummies/Cat+Photo.JPG

In fact it depends. When an AWS virtual machine needs to access an S3 object and the virtual machine and object reside in the same AWS region, Amazon does not impose any load on the road traffic that runs the object from S3 to EC2. However, if the virtual machine and the object are in different regions (traffic is directed to the Internet), AWS charges a penny per gigabyte, which can be costly for very large objects or for heavy use. For example, to resolve this problem, you can place multiple cubes containing duplicate objects in each region and change the names of the cubes to avoid conflicts, for example, renaming aws4dummies to aws4dummies_us_west and creating cubes with the same name in all others. cubes. regions

Given the importance of S3 for many applications, it is obvious that the service is reliable. The answer: it is reliable. In fact, because AWS has designed the service for 99.99% uptime, it should not be available for about 53 minutes per year. Durability is a complementary problem to availability: what is the reliability of S3 to never lose its object? The answer to this question is even more accurate: 99.999999999%. How does AWS achieve this high level of availability and sustainability? In a word, redundancy. Within each region, AWS stores multiple copies of each S3 object to prevent hardware from making access to an object impossible, or worse, by destroying a single copy. Even if a copy is not available due to a hardware failure, another copy is also available for access. If a hardware failure deletes a copy or renders it unavailable, AWS automatically creates a third copy to ensure the availability and durability of the object.

S3 cost

S3 has a simple cost structure: you pay for gigabytes of storage used by your objects. API calls to S3 are also expensive, which does not vary by volume. Finally, it pays for network traffic caused by the shipment of S3 objects. Storage costs start at $ 0.095 per gigabyte per month for the first terabyte and gradually decrease while total storage increases to $ 0.055 per gigabyte per month for more than 5,000 terabytes. The cost of API calls ranges from $ 0.01 per 1,000 requests (for PUT, COPY, POST or LIST calls) to $ 0.01 per 10,000 requests (for GET and all other requests). DELETE applications are free. The cost of data transfer, for transfers to or from an AWS region, varies in volume (as you can imagine). Data transfer is a gift: there is no cost for inbound network traffic that puts data into S3 storage. For outbound traffic, the first gigabyte of traffic is free. Then, rates become $ 0.12 per gigabyte up to 10 TB, with prices reduced depending on the scale. The price is reduced to $ 0.05 per gigabyte for traffic between 150 and 500 TB.

Amazon also offers reduced redundancy for S3 storage, which retains less copy of its data, and negotiates cost reliability. Redundant storage starts at $ 0.076 per gigabyte of storage and decreases to $ 0.037 per gigabyte in volumes greater than 5,000 TB. If S3 prices don't seem low enough, wait a bit. Amazon has consistently lowered prices for S3 storage since launching the service and continues to do so. The last price change before the publication of this book was published at the end of 2012 when S3 prices decreased by an average of 25%. If S3 prices don't seem low enough, wait a bit. Amazon has consistently lowered prices for S3 storage since launching the service and continues to do so. The last price change before the publication of this book dates from the end of 2012, when S3 prices decline an average of 25%. To update rates on S3, see http://aws.amazon.com/s3/pricing/.

Managing Volumes of Information with Elastic Block Storage (EBS)

Elastic Block Storage (EBS) is a volume-based storage that is not associated with any particular instance. instead, it is associated with instances to provide additional storage. Another way to say this is that an EBS volume is independent and has a different lifespan than EC2 instances. It can be linked.

at each instance to provide storage for that instance, but separates from the instance when it is finished. (If you've never worked with SAN storage, know the concept; if you haven't worked with SAN storage, don't worry, EBS is easy to understand.) However, you will definitely be working with EBS because they are extremely useful and resolves some important AWS limitations. The network-based EBS storage service is provided in volumes, which can be connected to an EC2 instance and used as a disk drive. Because the volume cannot be formatted, a file system must be installed (formatted) before it can be used. For example, if you want to attach an EBS volume to a Linux machine, you must first format the volume in one of the many file formats of the Linux file system and then mount it on the file system; which allows the operating system to access EBS. volume and read and write in the volume.

Because an EBS volume is network-based, its service life can be longer than any specific instance. Therefore, an EBS volume provides persistent storage that will not be lost when an instance ends or fails. The most common (but certainly not the only) use case of EBS is the file system of a database server. Database storage is located on the EBS volume, which must be associated with an instance that manages the database software so that the software can read and write to the EBS database storage. This process is a bit more complicated than using instance-specific storage, but has one major advantage: when using EBS, the application owner can ensure that the data is not prone to loss. from an interruption of the instance. Even if the instance fails, the volume of the EBS is immune from data loss. A new instance can be started, EBS volume can be associated, and the instance can restart database operations. The size of an EBS volume can be configured by the user and can range from 1 GB to 1 TB. The volumes are associated with accounts and are limited by default to 20 per account.

AWS generally sets predefined limits for different types of resources. It makes sense to prevent users from reserving resources and not using them. In the case of EBS, Amazon avoids allowing a customer to order 1,000 volumes and never uses 995. AWS, though extremely large, is not endless and resource reasoning is a means by which Amazon can provide its services. services to a large number of customers. However, if you need additional resources (regardless of your type, not just EBS), you can contact Amazon and tell them why you need more resources. Overall, Amazon is actively supporting people who really need additional resources and answering their questions. What if your large database requires more than 1 TB of storage? You can attach multiple EBS instances to the instance and distribute your file system in multiple volumes. (The tape here refers to being part of a multi-volume file system to increase the speed of reading and writing, rather than performance because all reads and writes are distributed on multiple hard drives.)

EBS reliability

EBS can improve the reliability of your applications because storage is independent of any specific instance (as noted in the previous section). Whatever happened with an instance, your data remains secure and protected. But what is the reliability of EBS? After all, why protect yourself from instance failures if the EBS service is not trusted? With EBS, Amazon has again used redundancy to increase reliability. Even though Amazon reveals little details about its service, it does indicate that many copies of each EBS volume are available at any time to protect against data loss due to hardware failures. If a disk drive containing an EBS volume becomes defective, Amazon makes a new drive available and copies the EBS volume data to the new drive to ensure it maintains the appropriate redundancy. Well EBS is very reliable, AWS suffered several major failures and the culprit managed to be at least twice EBS. What's going on with that?

The storage aspect of the EBS service is beyond doubt. In contrast, the EBS administration layer (or control plan, a geek term that means ... EBS administration layer) does not work well. The control plan is part of AWS smart infrastructure software and, unfortunately, problems can occur. Don't minimize problems with failures, but try to see them as the inevitable by-products of innovation represented by AWS. (EBS has only existed since 2008 and, believe it or not, AWS is only a few years old). In every new and different product, failure inevitably occurs. If you are concerned about interruptions, compare the reliability of AWS with that of your data center. This comparison generally helps put AWS failures into perspective and makes them less alarming.

EBS scope

AWS is generally organized into regions, each with one or more availability zones (AZs). With EBS, volumes reside in a single AZ in a given region. When you create an EBS volume, define to which AZ it puts (only) in a given region.

Of course, these instructions imply that any EC2 instance to mount and use this EBS volume must be in the same availability area. Such a configuration clearly presents a challenge. Although Amazon retains several copies of the EBS volume, they are all in the same AZ. Isn't it against the general orientation to make applications more robust by allowing you to correct (or work with) multiple AZs or even multiple AWS regions? The short answer is yes. If your application uses EBS volumes (and frankly, most of them), it is more difficult to follow AWS practices and make your applications work in multiple availability areas. Fortunately, there is a relatively simple way to solve this problem: use EBS snapshot.

Using EBS

To use EBS, simply create the volume using the AWS API or (most likely) using the AWS management console or third-party tool. As we noted earlier in this chapter, before you can use the volume, you must connect to a suitable operating system device in a running EC2 instance and then format it with a system file suitable for the system. exploitation The volume is ready to use. Now connected to an EC2 instance that manages as part of your preparation work and you can start using it immediately. When you decide to end the EC2 instance to which the

it simply separates the volume (again, via the AWS APS, the management console, or a third-party tool you use). The EBS volume enters the idle state, ready to be associated with a new EC2 instance at any time. In fact, it's even simpler than this: AWS unlocks the volume for you when you finish an EC2 instance, although good practices recommend it not be dependent on automatic disconnection.

Many people completely avoid manual connection / separation efforts and implement an automated approach by configuring the EC2 AMI launch process to automate the EBS connection process. (AMI refers to Amazon Machine Image, the format in which EC2 looks for instances when they are not running). Otherwise, many tools (from Amazon or third parties) do this work and avoid the need to implement in MAY. These tools start an AMI and execute the API commands to attack the volume.

EBS performance

Obviously, if EBS volumes are used for important application resources, such as databases, you may wonder if their performance is critical. How are they classified? Typical EBS performance is about 100 IOPS (I / O operations per second), and that's why EBS is designed. The question is what is the current performance of EBS.

In fact it depends. (You may not like this answer, but it's true. That's why.) EBS is network storage - it's far from the instance assigned to it. As a result, all data read and written in the volume must pass through the AWS network, and this is where things get complicated. When data must pass through a common resource, such as a network, it is subject to delays and interruptions caused by traffic from other applications. (That's true, by the way, of all data center environments, not just AWS). The traditional way to address this problem is to create a dedicated storage network (such as the term storage or SAN). Amazon, true to its roots as a low-cost carrier, has not set up a network dedicated to its EBS service, which has caused EBS's biggest complaint: uneven performance. Overall, the performance of EBS was not so bad, but worse, they tended to be extremely inconsistent due to the network congestion problem caused by other applications.

AWS faced this gap by expanding EBS service in mid-2012 with EBS-ready IOPS, designed to provide fast and predictable EBS performance. Expected IOPS provide guaranteed performance between 500 and 4000 IOPS on EBS volumes. This requires the use of optimized EBS instances, which provide dedicated performance, presumably for the use of a stored network. The same volume allocation strategy on multiple EBS volumes can be used with IOPS volumes provided to improve performance beyond the 4,000 Mbps limit. According to AWS prices, the use of IOPS provided is subject to higher costs. "Price EBS". You have to determine if the higher and more consistent EBS performance associated with provided IOPS is required and therefore worth it. The cost of the available IMP is not so high, but you can also keep it for a while and then move on to the provided IPS later if necessary.

File management with Glacier storage service

Glacier, launched in August 2012, is a storage service for a critical (but often mismanaged) need for computing: archive storage. In simple terms, file storage is a backup of all types of data. The best-known use of file storage involves server backups - complete dump of all data on the server drive. Today, of course, with the rise of NAS and SAN technologies, backups also include a backup of your storage device data. Glacier is designed to address the shortcomings of a number of traditional archiving solutions, none of which are quite satisfying, as they soon discovered. Tape file is the oldest solution for file storage. The data is written to a device that stores data on magnetic tapes, which are then sent off-site to ensure that no on-site disaster can erase all of the company's data, both live and archived. The Tape archive is packed with these issues:

- It is expensive: you usually need to use an offsite storage space and it costs money; The company sometimes also reduces the amount of data they archive. This strategy is tentative, but can become a major problem if the worst empire and its data disappear.
- This is a disadvantage: you have to move the tapes to the offsite storage location, and if you need to retrieve the information from the file, you must physically remove the tapes and restore from the tape.
- Slow: Obviously, sending and retrieving physical tapes is slow because you have to move them. A secondary aspect of slowness (writing and reading drawers) is a very slow process. Removing data from a tape can take hours (or even days, if your archive tapes are disorganized and you need to select multiple steps to find the desired data).

- Not safe: your tapes are out of place. Someone can get and read the data on the tape, putting your safety and privacy.

- This may not work: it is not known that the tape files are not working properly and the original write data to the tape may eventually deteriorate in memory.

A new way of archiving in recent years is based on the diminished cost of disk drives: when you archive the disk, backups are written from one real disk storage to another set of disk storage. Disk Archive The disk resolves some of the problems associated with tape problems, such as speed, but has its own (familiar) system of problems:

- Costs: Although archiving on tape may be expensive, archiving on disk is even more expensive. If you have a lot of data, backing up to other drives can be a huge cost, especially since a large amount of file storage is redundant: you have saved the file today and saved it today. Maintaining multiple copies of files on expensive media, such as disk, can increase costs. Fortunately, solutions come in the form of a deduction, which uses intelligent software and data structure to track parts of files that are changing, since only the modified bits are archived. This can reduce the amount of storage required to store data by up to 90%.

- Speed: Although disks work much faster than tapes, transferring data stored on the network to the remote file position can be a problem when you experience low internet and (possibly) low Internet speed. high network latency

- Reliability: This will not work: units may fail, such as stages. In general, the remote disk backup is isolated on a single disk disk and, in the event of failure of one of these disks,. . Here is your file.

- Glacier relies on the AWS infrastructure to provide file storage that responds to flaws in tape and disk solutions:

- It's economical: ice costs start at less than $ 0.02 per gigabyte of fuel storage. It is much cheaper than disk archive and even less expensive than tape archive, the old low-cost archive solution.

- It's durable: Glacier uses the S3 infrastructure, which means it can offer the same 99.999999999% durability as the S3 service. It is much more reliable than previous archiving solutions.

- Convenient: Simply send and retrieve Internet storage files, making it easy to extend your current backup solution to Glacier. Many of the latest business backup solutions offer deduplication capabilities. Therefore, if you use one of these solutions, you can be sure that you have the frozen archive option.

- Highly scalable: a storage file can reach 40 TB, which should be large enough for everyone.
- It's safe: data is transmitted by Glacier via SSL encryption, and the files themselves are encrypted when stored.
- It's fast: Data can be retrieved by Glacier in just five hours, which is significantly faster than tape-based file solutions that require file installation. And even though Glacier faced the same problem as the disk archive of sending data from the Internet, AWS has several solutions to this problem:
  - AWS Import / Export is a service that lets you send Amazon physical disk drives with your data. From the Amazon side, an Amazon employee downloads the data from the disk and adds it to AWS.
  - AWS Direct Connect is a service offered by Amazon in partnership with network service providers that establish a bandwidth connection between its facilities (or its own data center) and AWS. The connection can be up to 1 Gbps or 10 Gbps, which allows you to transmit or receive large amounts of data quickly.

Automating operational
tasks with Lambda

This chapter is about adding a new tool to your box. The tool we are talking about, AWS Lambda, is as flexible as a Swiss Army knife. You no longer need a virtual machine to run your own code because AWS Lambda provides runtime environments for Java, Node.js, C #, Python and Go.

All you have to do is implement a function, download its code and configure the runtime environment. Next, your code runs in a fully managed IT environment. AWS Lambda is well integrated with all parts of AWS, allowing you to easily automate the operational tasks of your infrastructure. We use AWS to automate our infrastructure on a regular basis. For example, we'll have to add and delete instances to a container cluster based on a custom algorithm, as well as to process and analyze log files.

AWS Lambda offers a maintenance-free and high availability computing environment. You no longer need to install security updates, replace faulty virtual machines, or manage remote access (such as SSH or

RDP) for administrators. Other than that, AWS Lambda is billed per call. Therefore, you do not have to pay for inactive resources while waiting for work (for example, an activity that is activated once a day).

In our first example, you will create a Lambda function that performs periodic status checks for your website. This will show you how to use the admin console and give you a plan to get started quickly with AWS Lambda. In our second example, you will learn how to write your own Python code and how to automatically implement a Lambda function using CloudFormation. Your Lambda feature automatically adds a tag to the newly launched EC2 instances.

Run your code with AWS Lambda

IT capability is available at various levels of abstraction in AWS: virtual machines, containers and functions. You've heard of the virtual machines that Amazon's EC2 service offers. Containers provide another layer of abstraction over virtual machines. We do not cover containers because that is beyond the scope of our book. AWS Lambda also provides good communication power: a runtime environment for small functions instead of a complete operating system or container.

When you are reading AWS Lambda, you may have found the term without a server. We define a serverless system that meets the following criteria:

- There is no need to manage and maintain virtual machines.
- A fully managed service that offers scalability and high availability.
- Invoices on demand and for consumption of resources.
- Call the function to run your code in the cloud.

AWS is not the only provider offering a platform without a server. Google (cloud functions) and Microsoft (Azure functions) are competitors in this area.

Run your code on AWS Lambda

To run your code with AWS Lambda, follow these steps:

1. Enter the code.
2. Upload your code and dependencies (such as libraries or modules).
3. Create a function that determines the runtime environment and configuration.
4. Call the function to run your code in the cloud.

You should not start a virtual machine. AWS executes your code in a fully managed communications environment. AWS Lambda currently offers runtime environments for the following languages:

- Java
- Node.js
- C #
- Python
- Come on

Comparison of AWS Lambda with virtual machines (Amazon EC2)

What is the difference between AWS Lambda and virtual machines? First, there is the granularity of virtualization. Virtual machines provide a complete operating system to run one or more applications. In contrast, AWS Lambda provides a runtime environment for a single function, a small part of an application. In addition, Amazon EC2 offers a virtual machine as a service, but you are responsible for executing it in a secure, scalable and highly available way. To do this, you need to put considerable effort into maintenance. On the contrary, AWS Lambda provides a fully managed runtime environment. AWS manages the underlying infrastructure for you and provides production-ready infrastructure.

Other than that, AWS Lambda is billed at runtime, not the second when a virtual machine is running. You do not have to pay for unused resources while waiting for applications or tasks. For example, running a script to verify the integrity of a website every 5 minutes on a virtual machine will cost you at least $ 4. Performing the same status check with AWS Lambda is free: it does not exceed the free monthly level of AWS Lambda.

Creating a Web site control with AWS Lambda

Are you responsible for the availability of a website or application? We try our best to make our blog cloudonaut.io accessible 24 hours a day, 7 days a week. An external health check acts as a safety net ensuring that we, not our readers, are the first to know when our AWS Lambda blog is the ideal choice for creating a website control site because it does not need computer resources. constant, but only every minute, for a few milliseconds. This section guides you through the health status settings of your AWS Lambda website. In addition to AWS Lambda, we use the Amazon CloudWatch service for this show. Lambda functions publish metrics to CloudWatch by default. Usually, it inspects metrics with graphs and creates alarms by setting dreams. For example, a metric can count failures when performing the function. In addition to this, Cloud-Watch provides events that can also be used to enable Lambda features. I use a calendar to post an event every 5 minutes here. The status control of your website is made up of three parts:

- Lambda function: Run a Python script that sends an HTTP request to your website (for example, GET https://cloudonaut.io) and verify that the response contains specific text (such as cloudonaut).

- Scheduled event: Activate the Lambda function every 5 minutes. This is comparable to the cron service on Linux.
- Alarm: monitors the number of failed status checks and notifies you by email when your website is unavailable.

Use the Admin Console to manually create and configure all required parts. In our opinion, this is an easy way to get acquainted with AWS Lambda.

Create a Lambda function

The following step-by-step instructions guide you through the configuration of a AWS Lambda-based website control. Open AWS Lambda in the management console:

https://console.aws.amazon.com/lambda/home. Click Create Function to start the Lambda Function Wizard.

AWS provides drawings for various use cases, including code and Lambda function configuration. We will use one of these plans to create a health check for the website. Select Blueprints and search for Canary Islands. Then click on the lambdacanary-python3 template header.

In the next step of the wizard, you must specify a name for your Lambda function. The role name must be unique in your AWS account, including in the current region of the eastern United States. UU. To call a function through the API, you must provide the function name, for example. Type web-health-check as the name of your Lambda function. Select Create a custom role to create an IAM role for your Lambda function.

To create a basic IAM role that gives your Lambda feature write access to CloudWatch logs:

1. Select Create a new IAM role.
2. Maintain the lambda_basic_execution role name.
3. Click the Allow button.
4. Select the Lambda Basic Run role from the drop-down list of existing roles.

You have already specified an IAM name and role for your Lambda function. You can configure the scheduled event that will activate your status control several times. We will use a 5 minute interval in this example.

1. Select Create new rule to create a scheduled event rule.
2. Enter the health-control-website as the name of the rule.
3. Enter a description that will help you understand what happens next.
4. Select Programmed Expression as the rule type.

5. Use the frequency (5 minutes) as a planning expression. 6 Remember to activate the trigger by running the box at the bottom.

Defines recurring things without needing a specific time using a rate planning expression ($ value $ unit). For example, you can activate a task every 5 minutes, every hour or once a day. The value $ must be a positive integer. Use minutes, minutes, hours, hours, days, or days as a unit. For example, instead of turning on the website integrity check every 5 minutes, you can use the fee (1 hour) as a programming expression to perform the state check every hour. Note that frequencies of less than one minute are not compatible.

Use CloudWatch to search the logs for your Lambda feature

How can I know if the status control of your website is working properly? How do you know if your Lambda function has been executed? It's time to see how to monitor a Lambda function. You must first learn how to access log messages for your Lambda function. Then it will create an alarm that will alert you if its function fails. Open the Monitoring tab in the detailed view of your Lambda function. You will find a table that shows the number of times your function has been invoked. Use the Reload chart button after a few minutes if the card does not show any invocation. To access your Lambda feature records, click View records in CloudWatch.

By default, its Lambda function sends log messages to CloudWatch. The group of records called / aws / lambda / website-health-check will be created automatically and collect the records for your function. Usually, a record group contains several record sequences, which allows you to scale. Click on Search Log Group to view log messages of all sequences in a single view. All registration messages are presented in the general description of the recording sequence. You may be able to find a successful control log message! indicating that the status check of the website has been completed and successful, for example.

Log messages appear after a few minutes. Reload the table if there are no log messages. It is convenient to be able to fetch log messages in a central location when debugging Lambda functions, especially if you write your own code. When using Python, you can use print instructions or use the journal to send log messages to CloudWatch out of the box.

What are the limitations of AWS Lambda?

Each call to your Lambda function must be completed within 300 seconds. This means that the problem you solve with your feature should be small enough to fit in 300 seconds. It is probably not possible to download 10

GB of S3 data, process the data and insert parts of the data into a database in a single call of a Lambda function. But even if your use case matches the 300 second restriction, make sure this is the case in all circumstances. Here's a brief history of one of our first serverless projects: We created a serverless application that preprocessed analytical data from news sites. Lambda functions usually process the data in less than 180 seconds. But in the U.S. election in 2017, the volume of analytical data exploded unexpectedly. Our Lambda functions could no longer be finished in less than 300 seconds. A spectacular brake on our serverless approach.

AWS Lambda provides and manages the resources required to perform its function. A new background execution context is created every time you implement a new version of your code, for a long time without a call or when the number of simultaneous calls increases. To create a new runtime context, AWS Lambda must download its code, initialize a runtime environment and upload its code. This process is called cold start. Depending on the size of the deployment package, the runtime environment, and its configuration, the boot boot can take a few milliseconds in seconds. Therefore, applications with very tight response time requirements are not good candidates for AWS Lambda. In contrast, there are many use cases where the additional latency caused by a cold start is acceptable. For example, the two examples in this chapter are not affected by a cold start. To minimize boot time, you must minimize the size of the deployment package, provide additional memory, and use a runtime environment such as Python, Node.js or Go instead of C # or Java. Another limitation is the maximum amount of memory you can provide for a Lambda function: 3008 MB. If your Lambda function uses more memory, its execution will be over.

It is also important to know that the processor and network capacity is also attributed to a Lambda function based on the memory provided. Therefore, if you are running computer or network functions on a Lambda function, increasing the allocated memory will probably improve performance.

At the same time, the default maximum size of the compressed implementation package (zip file) is 50 MB. When running your Lambda feature, you can use up to 500 MB of persistent disk space mounted on / tmp. See "AWS Lambda Limits" at http://docs.aws.amazon.com/.

Impact of the serverless pricing model

When you launch a virtual machine, you must pay AWS for each hour of operation, billed to the nearest second. It pays for the machines, no matter if you use the resource they provide. Even when no one is accessing your website or using your app, you pay for the virtual machine. It's totally different with AWS Lambda. Lambda is charged upon request. The costs are only incurred when someone accesses your website or uses your app. It's a game changer, especially for applications with irregular access patterns, or for frequently used applications.

Use case: Web application

A common use case for AWS Lambda is to create a backend for a web or mobile application. An architecture for a serverless web application typically consists of the following building blocks:

- Amazon API Gateway - Provides a scalable and secure REST API that accepts HTTPS requests from front-end or mobile app from your web application.
- AWS Lambda: Lambda functions are enabled by the API gateway. Your Lambda function receives the data from the request and returns it for response.
- NoSQL Object Store and Database: To store data requests, your Lambda features typically use additional services that include object storage or a NoSQL database, for example.

Want to start building AWS Lambda based web applications?

AWS Cloud Formation & OpsWork

Elastic Beanstalk is ideal for dynamic language applications that contain more than web and database levels, but what if your application includes additional levels to handle data caching and other logical processes or is language not dynamic? CloudFormation is an ideal solution for managing such applications. Horizontal scaling refers to the use of multiple computer instances to share workloads at one application level. Horizontal scaling is a technique for applications that support more than one instance. A different approach to solving this problem is called vertical scaling: use a more efficient instance to support higher loads. Vertical scaling is widely used, but it is the preferred solution for web applications for several reasons, including the fact that a (very) large instance exposes it to application failure. application instead of redundancy provided by several smaller instances. Also, a larger instance size is not available at some point. (And then what do you do?) Therefore, horizontal scaling is the most commonly implemented application design in computing cloud environments.

Finally, of course, you face a final challenge in managing complex webscale applications: human ineptitude, where you can see the downside of human creativity and ingenuity. Humans excel at developing new creations, but they're terrible at repetitively executing complex tasks. They make mistakes. And webscale applications bring out the worst in people, with lots of complicated configuration settings, arcane installation instructions, and detailed monitoring output that must be responded to. In short, webscale applications are increasingly difficult beasts to manage, and trying to do so via manual methods using the AWS Management Console — as useful as it is — is fraught with danger. Fortunately, Amazon has recognized this issue and developed a management tool that converts the management of webscale applications from an ongoing challenge to a process that leverages a template defining the components of an application, coordinating their launch, and even managing its ongoing response to changing workloads. That solution is CloudFormation.

CloudFormation operation is based on a template — in this particular case, a JSON text document. The template, which is the key to CloudFormation, serves as the basis for service creation and operation. The following list describes the various sections in the template that you'll use to define your application:

- Format: Format refers to the CloudFormation template version (not the file format or any other obvious term). Amazon clearly envisions evolving the service and wants the flexibility to change the template format to incorporate future developments. The company is unlikely to deprecate existing templates, so don't worry that your carefully created template will become obsolete. (Note: In CloudFormation terminology, the application is referred to as a stack, so keep this term in mind.)

- Description: Use this (text) section to describe the template and the application it manages. Think of it as a Comments section, where you can provide information for others as they use or modify your template.

- Parameters: These values, which are passed into CloudFormation at runtime, can be used to configure the application operated by the template. You may, for example, want to run CloudFormation templates in several Amazon regions; rather than create separate templates for each region, you can use one template and pass in a parameter to define in which region the template's application should run.

- Mappings: Here's where you declare conditional values. Think of this section as the one in which you set a variable used in the template to a particular value. For example, you may change the AMI ID that the template will launch, based on which region the "region" parameter is set to.

• Resources: This area describes the AWS resources used in the application and specifies the configuration settings. If you want the application to run all M1.Large instances, place that setting here. Of course, you can adjust the setting based on parameters and mappings instead, if you so choose.

• Outputs: These values are the ones you want returned in the event of a request to describe the template. The output may return the name of a template's author or the date of creation, for example.

CloudFormation templates are simple . . . but not easy. It's always that way when you move from manual to automated administration. Organizing a template to support all the different values and variables that are needed to operate a complex application isn't easy. It requires lots of iterative creation and testing. The benefit is that when the template operates properly, you save enormous amounts of time thereafter.

AWS OpsWorks

OpsWorks is Amazon's latest addition to its management tool library, released in March 2013. Though you can reasonably ask why AWS needs another AWS-supplied management tool, I can think of three reasons:

AWS customers want better support for the complete application lifecycle. They want it especially for incremental development and faster transitioning to production, both of which are now typical of applications. The other AWS management tools (Elastic Beanstalk and CloudFormation) tend to work on the assumption that the application code to be deployed is static and complete.

The demand for shorter application rollouts has developed a new IT set of practices and tools. The practices are DevOps, a portmanteau (combination) word — or mash-up, if you prefer — that indicates the integration of development and operations in an effort to streamline the entire application lifecycle and shorten the time it takes to convert an application into a product. A couple open source products have become core parts of the DevOps movement, and one of them, Chef, is part of OpsWorks.

Though many technology employees are perfectly happy to work with text- and API-based tools, many would find complex tasks easier to implement with a visual tool. Let's face it — JSON (particularly, complex JSON files like those required by CloudFormation) are challenging, to say the least.

OpsWorks terminology

Some of the terminology used by OpsWorks (stack, instance, application) may sound familiar to you, but OpsWorks often puts its own twist on a term's meaning. Here's a mini-dictionary of its terms:

• Stack: A complete application that spans multiple tiers and instances, which is consistent with CloudFormation terminology. Application-level elements, like instance blueprints (which are definitions of what software components are installed on a specific instance within a stack), user permissions, and AWS resources (S3 buckets and Elastic Load Balancers, for example) are defined at the stack level.

• Layer: Layer defines how to create and configure a set of instances and related resources, such as EBS volumes. Most people would refer to a layer as an application tier — like an application tier, a layer performs one well-defined set of functionality within the context of an application. For example, a layer may operate a PHP environment to run application logic. To reduce the development burden on AWS users, Amazon provides a number of preconfigured layers — such as Ruby, PHP, HAProxy (a load balancer), memcached, and MySQL — that you can either use as is or extend to suit your particular needs. These layers can be combined to form a complete OpsWorks application.

- Instance: Instances become members of a layer and are configured to meet the needs of the layer in which they operate. Configuration includes setting its size and the location of the availability zone in which it operates. An instance can also be made part of an Auto Scaling Group to support erratic application workloads.

- Applications: The application-specific code that you write to perform the functionality you wish to implement. The other portions of OpsWorks exist to support you in deploying and running your application code. To place your application code on the instances within layers, you take advantage of the wonder that is Chef. (In fact, OpsWorks uses Chef to install its necessary software, which it does before it turns to installing your application code.)

- Monitoring, logging: To monitor the complex collection   of   instances,   components,   and configurations that is part of today's applications, OpsWorks implements CloudWatch, performs extensive logging, and also monitors application environments, using the open source tool Ganglia.

Using OpsWorks

The correct way to wrap your mind around OpsWorks is to approach it from the top down:

1. Figure out the overall architecture of the application you want to implement and operate. This "whiteboard design" stage presents a high-level overview of your application.

2. Drill down to the layer level and assign specific responsibilities to each layer. For example, make sure that your application's Memcached layer will be responsible for caching user information to reduce database reads. To do so, you define the functionality you'll need. Don't assume that you have to arrange for each layer and for all the code needed for that layer. You can leverage AWS functionality so that if you need, say, a key-value store as one layer in your application, you can use DynamoDB for it.

3. Determine what functionality needs to reside in an instance to perform its role within the layer. If part of your application transcodes images (transforms

them from one digital format to another, in other words), you would want to incorporate a Chef recipe that defines and configures the appropriate instance resources and connects to the AWS Elastic Transcode service to perform the transcoding. You would also want to include a recipe to install your own code that manages receiving the images, submits them to Elastic Transcode, receives the bucket name in which the transcoded image is stored, and returns that information to the image submitter.

4. Create the OpsWork stack by defining the different layers, the instance roles within the layers, and the necessary configuration for each type of instance.

Just as CloudFormation requires a lot of iterative testing to evaluate whether the application definition is correct and operates properly, so too does OpsWorks. Recognize that getting an OpsWorks stack ready requires a fair amount of work, which is repaid over time as you repeatedly create the stack and run your application. OpsWorks is so new that no one has a lot of experience with it "in the field," as they say, but I expect that most people will approach it like they approach CloudFormation: Walk through a design process as just outlined; and then use an existing AWS-supplied resource as a jumping-off point, and modify it to support the requirements of the design.

AWS Database

A database is software that can read digital information and then reliably store it in a structured format, so that information can be effectively returned in useful formats and combinations. Imagine that your company keeps records of all your customers, including their names, addresses and previous purchases. From time to time, you probably want to access this information. You may need an address to submit an invoice, or you can analyze your data to find correlations between addresses and purchase patterns.

The world of data can become very complex, very fast. In practice, however, it is fair to say that most projects can be successfully served by one of two database models: relational (SQL) and NoSQL.

Relational databases

If you need to organize your data to precisely define the relationships between different categories of information, you can use a relational database. Imagine a company that, for example, has to manage its employees based on their job, payment method and their health insurance status. The data of each employee are included in each of these categories, but at the same time they may not be accessible to other users beyond what is individually needed. Relational databases are often managed by some kind of SQL standard. SQL is an acronym for the structured query language, whose "structured" part tells the essence of the story. A SQL database (which includes Oracle, MySQL, PostgreSQL, Microsoft SQL Server, and most recently, Amazon Aurora) consists of tables that contain records (or, as some call them), rows. The records consist of individual values called fields.

Here, the database contains records identified by the numbers 1 and 2, and each record contains fields consisting of a name, an address, and a purchase amount. The main advantage of this type of solid structure may be that it allows for high levels of predictability and reliability because carefully defined rules can be applied to all transactions that affect your data. For example, you can apply restrictions on how users of an application can access the database, to ensure that two users do not try to write changes to a single record at the same time. times (which could lead to data corruption).

NoSQL databases

The climate is changing. In all segments of the IT world, data is produced, used and analyzed at volumes and at unexpected speeds when the first relational database was built more than a generation ago. Imagine, for example, developing a wholesale business that has to deal with constantly changing product descriptions and inventory information for tens of thousands of items; This data, in turn, needs to be integrated with sales, shipping and customer service operations. In this case, you probably want to use a NoSQL database (such as AWS DynamoDB): Extremely flexible relationships between NoSQL data elements make it much easier to integrate data stored in different clients and in different formats. This facilitates the management of fast growing data sources.

Despite what you may think, some argue that NoSQL is not synonymous with No SQL or Not SQL, but not just SQL. This means that these databases can sometimes support operations similar to SQL. In another

In other words, you can sometimes request a NoSQL database to provide functionality similar to what you might expect from a relational database. For more complete information on NoSQL and its integration into the broader spectrum of database models, the AWS document "What is NoSQL?" It may be helpful: http://aws.amazon.com/nosql.

How you choose

The architecture of the database you choose for a project will often depend on the specific needs of your application. For example, if you are carrying out financial transactions and, because of the imperative need for absolute accuracy and consistency, it is essential that a single disk can never contain more than one value, you will probably opt for a platform. Relational Imagine the chaos that would result if all the money in a particular account were withdrawn from two sessions of simultaneous customers. On the other hand, suppose you are an organization of an online multiplayer game. If the user allows to quickly update the data points can make a difference in the player's experience, and an occasional typo will not cause a zombie apocalypse, they will want to consider NoSQL.

Infrastructure drawing: Who owns your database?

Here are some reasons why you may want to install and run an outdated database (on your own dedicated server):

Security: Even if you generally want the content of a website or application to be accessible to anyone who wants to browse the Internet, this will not be the case with your database. As far as possible, it should be protected from external access. Think about what might happen if everything Google knew about its billions of customers was exposed to the general public (it's awesome that Google knows). To isolate your various resources into completely separate machines, it is much easier to open what needs to be opened and close the rest. Databases often have access profiles that differ greatly from applications. Therefore, they fit perfectly into this type of separation.

Accessibility to data: It is common to start multiple servers in one application. This may be because they all provide a single service, but they can generally duplicate their content to protect against server failure or to meet growing user demand. However, when multiple application servers use the same data, it is often a good idea to separate your database.

Hardware: Web or application servers often consume computer resources differently from databases. The former can rely heavily on the power of a powerful multi-core processor, while the latter can succeed with high-speed SSDs. It's always good to let everyone play with their favorite games.

Software: Suppose your application requires a Windows server, but you want your data to be stored on a Linux computer. Although, technically, this can be done using the magic of virtualization, you may want to avoid the additional complications of running both operating systems on a single server.

AWS RDS: Finally we return AWS to Learn AWS in one month for lunch. The Amazon Relationship Database Service (RDS) provides a fully managed database solution that can be easily integrated with EC2-based applications. The management means that Amazon supports all administrative and hardware issues and provides you with a unique Internet address (called an endpoint) to access the resource. AWS offers you a guaranteed, available, replicated (saved to protect against data loss in the event of a failure) and correct (MySQL, Oracle, Aurora, etc.) database (the software is the newest and most available)). You can only do these features by downloading your database.

Migrate your database to RDS

Assuming that you have chosen a RDS-based management database that you have always wanted for your birthdays, you need to find out how to create one or, in this case, how to use the database for which you have already created it. WordPress project and migrate to RDS without having to rebuild. What it will do to make it work:

1. Create a usable copy of your existing database, which by default is already full and active. This is called database dump.
2. Go to the AWS console to create an RDS instance. Make sure that a secure connection between your EC2 instance and your EC2 instance is possible.
3. Upload your saved image to the RDS database server.

NOTE If your database is currently active and you do not want to miss current transactions, you must prepare carefully for this process, which will be beyond the scope of this manual. The AWS Database Migration Service (https://aws.amazon.com/dms/) is an excellent tool to facilitate the transition.

AWS Networking

Networks are a big problem in the AWS scheme. Without this, none of your AWS instances could send and receive network traffic. However, on the networks, as with all other AWS design elements, Amazon has implemented a clearly ingenious but equally different solution from traditional solutions known to most users. And AWS has taken the road less traveled, for the same reasons it innovated in other aspects of its design: expanding and promoting automation. When Amazon decided to expand its AWS offering, it thought it was "big," really big. In fact, Amazon's vision is always focused on a much bigger future than the current one. Even though it started out as an online booklet, it is still set to become a general (and extremely profitable) online marketer. Their efforts to sell books work well because it was a practical category that made relatively little consumer resistance to using the (still unknown to date) support of e-commerce. This anticipation strategy allowed AWS designers to create an offer that could go beyond anything existing in the industry.

You will be surprised to learn that networks have become a major obstacle to implementing the Amazon plan. However, this should come as no surprise that Amazon has developed a unique approach to networking in a cloud computing environment that easily forgets this obstacle.

Laying the basics of networks

When computers communicate, they do so via a network. For the vast majority of IT operations worldwide, this conversion activity is performed over a TCP / IP network. The TCP / IP network standard uses the concept of layers to illustrate the flow of communication. In this model, layers are numbered 1, 2, and 3:

- Physical layer (layer 1): This is associated with the cables installed in the office or the way your wireless access point communicates with the wireless card on your computer.

- Data link level (layer 2): controls the flow of data between network entities (hosts, domain names, subnets, etc.) that reside on the same network; This local area network (LAN) is dedicated to a single organization. These entities usually have a network interface card (NIC), each with a unique identifier: its MAC (Media Access Control) address. Layer 2 explains how two entities with MAC addresses can send data to each other. (Note that this data is sent using a network card, a convenient hardware component that is maintained on a server).

- Network layer (layer 3): controls the flow of data between network entities residing in different networks. In this WAN, users communicate over multiple wireless LANs and cannot rely on a connection established over the same local physical layer. Layer 3 works most often using Internet Protocol (IP), which uses a logical address scheme (called, logically, IP addresses) to communicate. IP addresses generally have four digits, say 10.1.2.3, where each digit is represented by an eight-bit data set. The screen uses points to separate 8-bit segments, and the four segments are expected to represent a hierarchy; that is, part 10.1 of the address must contain a set of network devices that reside in part 10.1 of the address. For example, your ISP has a wide range of addresses because it can control all addresses starting with, for example, the number 16. Two special cases, the high-level numbers 10 and 192, do not represent an IP address. which can be publicly rebuked. addresses but are used for private addresses. (Cannot be dragged via public Internet). Therefore, many entities can use these high-level numbers in their own data centers as a kind of private identifiers.

There are other top layers in a TCP / IP network, but the most important ones in a cloud computing network are layers 2 and 3, where the challenge is to be a cloud computing provider. You may ask, "How do virtual machines send and receive network traffic?" After all, they are virtual and do not have a hardware network adapter. Of course, the answer is that they have a virtual network card (sometimes called a VNIC), a software construct through which the virtual machine sends and receives network traffic. The virtualization supervisor manages the assignment of these packets to and from the physical network adapter that connects to the physical network in the data center and communicates.

Virtual LANS: keeps your data private

In a shared network environment (and remember that this is precisely what a cloud computing provider offers), how can you assure a user that their data is not accessible to another user? Obviously, one solution is to create separate physical networks and allow each user account to have its own local network. However, it would be a logistics burden (and extremely expensive). In addition, this method requires that each user has their router to the outside world to communicate all their Layer 3 traffic to other external users.

Routers have been upgraded to provide local area virtual networks (VLANs) that exist essentially in connecting larger network sections to specific users. In this VLAN, traffic passes through layer 2; All traffic to other parts of the network or shared internet goes through Layer 3. What is the interest of Layer 2 or 3 traffic? Why would anyone care about the layer that communicates? For many years, Layer 2 traffic would work faster because the network switches that processed it didn't have to look at the packet to determine where to send it. It could transmit the initial packet to all the devices on the local network, observe the responder and its MAC address, and then transmit the traffic directly to the MAC address.

Layer 3, on the other hand, needed to examine the packet to determine the IP address for which it was intended, by finding the address in an IP / MAC address mapping table and then sending the packet to the MAC address. . Research has altered network performance. The switches are now robust enough that over IP / MAC research is trivial; In other words, not enough to really improve performance. Therefore, the reason for having VLANs in a cloud environment is that it can separate user traffic, not improve performance.

Most hosting companies use VLAN technology to assign a virtual LAN to each client so that their computers are separate from the computers of other clients. This strategy, which provides customers with a secure network solution, tells them that their network traffic is safe from interception. In general, most hosting companies do all the work associated with manually assigning and configuring VLANs when setting up the account. A network administrator accesses the provider's router and configures a VLAN for the new client. The client computers are placed in the newly configured VLAN and the network traffic path for them. Since hosting companies have resorted to cloud computing, they have almost always adopted the practice of creating a VLAN for each new client, with new virtual machines assigned in the VLAN address space. This VLAN can be configured manually or automatically, depending on the cloud infrastructure of the provider.

Continuous use of VLANs in these environments makes sense, especially since many providers offer hosting and cloud computing from the same institution; Using a consistent VLAN approach allows sharing of resources and simplicity of infrastructure. However (is this not always the case?), Using VLAN for cloud compression has some disadvantages:

- Delay in account configuration: Cloud computing providers that continue to create and configure VLANs manually require a delay in the initial installation of the client account. Many customers find this delay inconvenient; others see it as a barrier to using this cloud computing provider.

- Limit the number of VLANs that a router can handle: This limitation can be resolved by using multiple routers, but it imposes complexity on the provider's infrastructure.

- Limit the number of computers that could be connected to a specific VLAN: Although many clients are not affected, this limit is an unacceptable problem for web-based applications that may need hundreds (or even thousands) of computers.

Amazon's alternative to VLANs

Since Amazon wants to avoid the scale limitations of VLAN technology in its cloud service, the VLAN approach is obviously unacceptable for the following reasons:

- Limiting the number of VLANs will limit the number of customers Amazon can support with its AWS service. When Amazon first defined its plans for AWS, it expected hundreds of thousands of customers to finally use AWS. Therefore, this limitation was too restrictive.

- Limiting the number of computers a client could have on the same VLAN limits the number of instances that can be used in their applications. Amazon itself has experience with applications that shoot hundreds or even thousands of instances, so expect customers to do so too. A solution that limits the amount of computers used by individual customers is clearly unacceptable.

Because of this, Amazon has designed its network very different from the traditional approach and has implemented a network design with the following features:

- Use of Layer 3 technology across infrastructure: All traffic is directed to the IP address, without the use of the Layer 2 MAC address.
- It is imperative that an IP address is assigned to each instance and that all traffic to that instance is driven by the IP address: this is true whether the traffic originates from AWS or externally, without exception.
- No support or support for VLAN technology: In each region, Amazon has one or more IP address ranges, and IP addresses are randomly assigned to client instances at those intervals. The corollary of this approach is that all AWS IP addresses are those of Amazon and not those of the customer. For example,

if a customer decides to move their website from their data center to AWS, the website will have a new IP address.

AWS networks are often described as completely flat: all traffic is based on an iPad address and the IP address assigned to an instance does not involve any hierarchy. There is no doubt that managing a landline imposes challenges and complexity on Amazon, but simplifies the use of the customer's network. As a specific VLAN client has not been created or configured for them, the account setup process is extremely streamlined, so that the entire process can be automated to a greater extent than others. cloud providers, more traditional. In addition, because customers are not separate in the assigned VLANs, it is much easier to multiply and reduce the number of cases a customer uses: customers can simply request additional instances and Amazon can launch a new one. instance and assigns a much larger IP address. group global IP addresses and return the IP address of the instance to the client.

The IP address may be very different from the one assigned to the client, but since all traffic is direct based on the IP address, discontinuity in the range of addresses is not a problem. Many experienced network administrators, familiar with the network practices that computer organizations and hosting providers often use, find Amazon's approach of concern. Overall, they have worked hard to design and adjust network configurations for maximum performance, and believe Amazon's smart-scale design should penalize performance terms.

Stay AWS IP

Addressing Unlike other cloud providers, which assign a fixed address range to virtual machines hosted on client-assigned VLANs, AWS dynamically assigns IP addresses from its own range of IP addresses.

There is no IP address permanently assigned to a client account and a server launched by a particular image can be assigned an IP address today and a different IP address tomorrow. This moving IP address may seem confusing. So, let me describe in more detail how AWS organizes your IP address. For starters, each instance of the network has its own virtual network interface card, or VNIC, a software build that mimics the functionality of a NIC hardware. The Xen hypervisor in AWS allocates traffic between the VNIC of each instance and the actual hardware network adapter on the physical server where the Xen hypervisor runs.

AWS assigns two IP addresses to the VNIC of an instance: a public IP address and a private IP address. The last one is at 10.X.X.X. This is a range designed not to travel on the Internet and allows private traffic to data centers.

Having two IP addresses means that each instance can send and receive the external traffic to AWS at a publicly available IP address. In AWS, instances can communicate with each other using the private IP address assigned to them. In other words, if I have two servers, one to which AWS has assigned 10.1.2.3 and the other 10.1.2.4, these servers can exchange traffic with 10.XXX addresses instead of the public IP address that AWS has assigned. This traffic is not carried via the public Internet; instead, it is limited to AWS.

This division between private and public IP addresses may seem like an academic distinction: after all, if traffic contains TCP packets, who cares about the address to which they are sent, whenever the instance receives them? However, the difference between the two IP addresses is quite important for your AWS invoice because the traffic on the local AWS network (10.XXX addresses, in other words) is much less expensive than the traffic sent to the IP addresses. . public. To illustrate the difference, traffic between two availability zones in the same region costs $ 0.01 per GB, while traffic between two availability zones is sent to a public IP address (and therefore routed through the Internet. public).) costs 0, 12 USD per GB. 12 times more!

The essential aspect of this concept is the network traffic sent by an instance: all incoming traffic (the traffic receiving an instance) is free, both of the AWS and of a public Internet network. Outbound traffic (traffic sent by an instance), on the other hand, is economical if your destination resides in the same AWS region and generates high network rates if the network address is outside AWS.

Each instance has a unique public IP address, while instances that reside in different regions share private IP addresses. The reason is that private IP addresses cannot be accessed from outside the local environment and the same address can be used securely in many regions because there is no way to access an instance with their private IP address. from outside. Therefore, the instance of Regions 1 and 2 have the same private IP address: 10.1.2.3.

And, as if this concept is not complicated enough, Amazon has withdrawn its honors of regional communication between AWS, dramatically and literally as it writes this chapter. For example, the cost of traffic between the eastern US. UU. Other AWS regions increase from $ 0.12 per gigabyte to $ 0.02 per gigabyte, a reduction of 83%. Users now have three options for network traffic:

- Intra-regional: traffic between AWS resources in a particular region (for example, the eastern United States); Free to send and receive traffic.
- Interregional: traffic between AWS resources in different regions. For each resource, all the traffic it receives is free, but the traffic it transmits carries costs (certainly low).
- extra-regional: traffic between an AWS resource and a non-AWS resource; traffic to the AWS resource is free and any traffic sent from the resource incurs full traffic loads.

The cost of the network is based on the total gigabytes of traffic sent in a month and the price per gigabyte. The first gigabyte of traffic per month is free; Traffic from 2 gigabytes to 10 terabytes per month is $ 0.12 per gigabyte. As traffic increases by more than 10 terabytes per month, the cost per gigabyte decreases. at 350 terabytes per month, one gigabyte costs just $ 0.05; Above this level, you are invited to contact AWS to (presumably) sign a customized price agreement.

AWS Direct Connect

The fact that all network traffic between AWS and non-AWS resources passes through the public Internet is a major problem: despite the fact that Internet connectivity is offered by very large service providers who have invested a lot of money in their networks. stay. , The levels of bandwidth and latency available to end users are highly variable and may be unacceptable. The seeds of this kind of problem existed at the birth of the Internet. By its nature, the Internet is a shared network in which millions of computer packages are mixed when they are sent over the network. The package on your computer is in competition with everyone else. The advantage is that a shared network is much cheaper (save emails and Facebook); The disadvantage is that the performance and performance of a shared network are much less predictable. For you and me, it doesn't matter.

If a Netflix video runs a bit slow, it's not a terrible problem, and many of the things we do are not affected too much by network problems. For example, email generally works the same way, with network transfers of up to 1,000%. For businesses, though, inconsistent network performance can be a big problem. When you can't watch a video, take care of your business and do something else. However, when an employee cannot see a security video, their ability to work may be impaired, and paying someone who cannot work is a big problem.

From the point of view of many companies, another problem can be caused: Internet traffic travels through a shared network and can allow inappropriate access to company data. For some companies or certain types of data, sending traffic on a publicly accessible network is prohibited. Amazon solves the problem of public Internet traffic with Direct Connect: it allows a user to put a private circuit between their data center and AWS to allow traffic through a dedicated network connection, without using public Internet. Dedicated Direct network connections can be established by AWS to an enterprise data center or public operator, such as Equinix. The company that requires the Direct Connect network connection may have its servers located on the public operator's site or have a second network connection between the public operator and its data center. Obviously, a dedicated network connection solves the problem of packet confidentiality. A company using Direct Connect can be sure that their network traffic is safe from prying eyes. Additionally, you can deploy a virtual private network (VPN) between your AWS instances and your own data center to improve data security. (Describing virtual private networks and how it works is beyond the scope of this book, but suffice it to say that they use smart software to encrypt data that travels through secure networks, such as the public Internet.)

Amazon offers two levels of Direct Connect bandwidth: 1 Gbps and 10 Gbps. The first should be sufficient for most connection needs; The latter is sufficient for all high performance calculations except the most demanding, and is the highest level of performance available in AWS. Direct Connect comes with an AWS-type financial agreement: use Direct Connect only when you need it and pay only when you use it. The direct connection costs $ 0.30 per hour for the 1 Gbps variant and $ 2.25 per hour for the 10 Gbps variant. As you can imagine, it doesn't pay for inbound network traffic, and outbound traffic varies between $ 0.03 and $ 0.11 per gigabyte, depending on the region. Although bandwidth and Direct Connect prices are extremely attractive, AWS connection needs to be completed by one of Amazon's Direct Connect partner sites. Your traffic must reach one of these locations, which you can obtain by hosting your servers in a carrier or by paying for a dedicated bandwidth circuit from your data center to the partner's location. The additional costs incurred should not affect the value (or profitability) of the Direct Connect offer.

Managing AWS Costs

Amazon is famous for its ability to manage AWS on a large scale, its efficient use of automation and its history of reducing costs. However, Amazon's ability to manage AWS effectively and at low cost does not automatically mean that the resources it manages AWS are efficient and economical. In fact, using AWS inefficiently is not difficult, since you can easily obtain AWS resources, you can end up using AWS less efficiently than local computing resources. You might think, "Hey, it's easy to start a server," thinking it only costs $ 0.06 per hour and forget (or not bother) to shut it down. However, like a shock robe, small amounts can be added to a useless resource source.

These losses can be a big problem when an organization can have dozens of applications and hundreds of cases running on AWS. The increase in AWS services exacerbates this problem, given the amount of additional services to monitor. However, do not worry: this chapter explains the tools available to solve cost efficiency and problems. Also give some general tips on how to keep your AWS running efficiently and profitably.

Amazon imposes full transparency on the billing of its services, unlike most of its competitors who publish statements on their websites: "To find out about rates, contact a sales representative to find out your requirements ". (You will never know what these owners charge unless you submit them to a sales pitch). Amazon should be praised for having experienced these hostile practices and for facilitating the search for specific charges. Amazon should also be praised for its innovation in the implementation of new services. Just at the time of writing this book, it has implemented two new basic services and a lot of small improvements to its existing services. The company should also be commended for creating its EC2 reserved instance offer, which reduces the total cost of ownership (TCO). And, of course, Amazon deserved praise for offering volume-based pricing reductions.

The challenge of tracking Amazon's costs has resulted from all this complacent and enjoyable behavior. In simple terms, Amazon has rapidly developed a variety of services and price structures that are very difficult to try to understand all the costs incurred in your account. it's even worse when you have complex applications that use many different AWS resources at many levels, not to mention trying to figure out how to load the temporary application (which usually drives the resource scale) temporarily using additional resources to ensure adequate performance. of the application) affects the costs.

During its short life, AWS has evolved from a limited set of services with a limited set of options to a wide range of services and options that are much more difficult to track and contradict. Total cost of ownership easy. Obviously, you need to understand how to use your resources, understand the templates and analyze what you can do to ensure your AWS costs are as basic as possible. Additionally, you will not want to reduce your costs to the extent that it will negatively affect the availability or performance of your application.

Do you feel tired of this cost and performance battle? Fortunately, help is near. Continue reading

Taking advantage of cost and usage

What is the importance of managing your use and the costs of AWS? It is very important. Cloudyn, one of the leading companies in the field of AWS usage analytics, has learned to show some customer statistics to highlight common usage patterns of AWS and, of course, to describe the challenges that can occur when users do not drive. no. your use of AWS reflexively.

Cloudyn took a sample of 400 customers and analyzed the use of AWS by these companies in January 2013. In a discussion of their results, the company said it had conducted a similar survey last year and found some results. similar. Therefore, the results of January 2013 may be considered representative. how many companies use (and abuse) AWS. Companies primarily represent business customers, which means that the population interviewed represents the end users of the computer, not the suppliers. In addition, companies tend to be larger, as opposed to small start-ups.

A large percentage of the survey group spends less than $ 50,000 a year, but of the total amount spent, this group represents only 4%. At the other end of the spectrum, only 4 percent of the study group spends more than $ 1 million a year on AWS, but these companies account for more than half of AWS's total spending across the group. . Surprisingly, a higher percentage of the survey group spends more than $ 1 million a year, ranging from $ 500,000 to $ 1 million.

In this distribution, network traffic falls into the Other category, so you don't see it specifically identified. Frankly, those numbers surprised me. I was expecting more charges for S3 and am amazed that EC2 represents a large portion of the total. However, we can conclude that:

- EC2 will represent a significant proportion of your total expenses. Pay particular attention to the use of your EC2 to ensure that it is used as efficiently as possible. I will advise on this later in the chapter on things.

- Although AWS services listed as Other (such as SQS and SNS) do not appear to be expensive, they account for almost 20% of the total annual expense of surviving businesses. These services will probably be used more than is generally recognized, and their use can lead to significant costs. Individually, the "other" AWS services may not be expensive, but in general they are important.

The pricing model you choose is far more important than it seems at first glance. Many people find that the hourly rate for a single instance of EC2 on demand is so low that it is not worth ordering the reserved instance. Also, many people do not know how long they use a particular example, so they avoid reserved instances because they feel that they are making a long-term commitment without knowing it is worth it.

If you're even more adventurous, use unique instances where AWS allows you to bid on unused resources. The disadvantage of using specific examples is that you can never be sure of getting EC2 instances at your offer price. On the other hand, you can try launching a spot price, and if there is no instance available at the offer price, go to an instance on demand. Pinterest, the extremely successful and often unusual service that allows you to "gather and organize everything you love," is a great user of unique instances as a strategy to reduce AWS total spend. The site's commitment to identifying instances is so strong that

embedded in your application code. The application always tries to start a one-time instance (via the AWS SDK). If a one-time instance is not available, your code changes to a second initial call for an on-demand instance. Cloudyn also looked at how the survey team used AWS resources and identified two other important results:

- 16% of Elastic Block Store volumes were not attached to an instance. The volume was created but not used at any time during the one-month monitoring period. Although it is possible that some of these volumes could be used sometime outside of that period, most are probably volumes that were previously used, now forgotten or abandoned, even if they are not used, the client is always He prays for them.
- The average CPU load in all EC2 cases was only 19%. In other words, over 80% of processing capacity has been wasted. It makes sense to have some degree of safety for prickly loads, but 80% represents a large amount of waste; again, even if capacity is not used,

it is still billed. That is, AWS users pay for something they do not use.

- This list explains the main points of this extremely interesting probe:

- The use of AWS is excellent. Even if you're not a big AWS user, you probably leave it behind, especially if you follow a common anecdotal pattern: start with a few, with a casual use of AWS, maybe a quick application prototype - and find out how easy it is obtain. resources and being productive, it grows its use rapidly so that its use of infrastructure is relatively large.

- EC2 is likely to account for the vast majority of your expenses. Many organizations believe that the ease of availability of IT resources, especially in relation to the extensive provisioning cycle of their online infrastructure, gives EC2 an almost convincing appeal. And don't forget that for companies under competitive pressure, EC2's immediate delivery process allows for market agility, which is very popular in today's global economy.

- Despite the importance of EC2, other AWS services will undoubtedly be a large part of your total spend. Pay attention to how you use one of the other AWS services. It is equally important to work on understanding them (using a valuable resource like this book) so you can better evaluate how to use them to create better applications and more agility.

- Monitor your AWS usage habits to make sure you get the most out of what you pay for and don't lose AWS resources. Historically, given the difficulty of obtaining resources, many IT organizations have over-supplied their resources, believing that it was better to buy too much and avoid the tedious process rather than risk by surprise. and they will repeat an unfortunate experience. In the AWS world, where getting IT resources (or freeing them) is trivial, this "overbought" behavior is not necessary; Worse, it costs you real money because you pay for AWS all the time, even if you do nothing with the resources.

Managing Your AWS Costs

Now that you know that AWS is a big problem, that you probably have a lot to use and that it is difficult to manage profitably, you will probably want to guide you to make sure you make your money. AWS worthy. You're in the right place, so here are some good practice tips:

√ Design applications must be scalable, both up and down. Use several smaller EC2 examples instead of a smaller number of larger instances. This ensures that your full IT capability adapts to the extra application load, so you have the right software at all times.

- Follow a "failed" application management strategy. This term, coined by Forrester analyst James Staten, means that you should seek to have just the right amount of IT resources available at any one time, and you must aggressively reduce your IT resources as the application load decreases. . This simple and immediate AWS performance feature supports this feature because if the application load increases, you can easily add resources to your application. And if you've followed the above recommendation to make your application scalable, your application easily scales to a growing or shrinking pool of resources.

- Operate Auto Scale groups. Operating load is one of the challenges in following the "low and low" strategy (and the "up and down" complement to meet the growing demands of applications). For each instance to start or end, an operator must perform certain functions: adding or subtracting the instance from a resource group, connecting to other instances, and eventually adding a load balance to the mix. To handle this load, use Auto Scaling, AWS groups that respond to this challenge. Set up your app from the start and let Amazon take care of dynamically escalating your resource pool while you have a cup of coffee.

- Take advantage of an AWS management tool from Amazon or a third party. Auto Scaling groups are great for managing EC2, but as the survey points out, many other AWS resources are used. AWS management tools can reduce the operational costs of managing these other resources, such as SQS and RDS. (Less work and more coffee break for you!)

- Run application load tests to help with your financial modeling. When you load your application with simulated traffic, you can see the resources used by large volumes. You will then be able to see if it is likely to expand the use of certain services enough to obtain volume reductions based on volume. On the contrary, it also indicates that, during larger application loads, you use some services unnecessarily and can change the design of your application to reduce the use of these services and save money. Of course, I advise you to do load tests to ensure better application robustness; This is an added benefit of load and performance tests. Various open source load / performance test products and services are available. The one I like is SOASTA (www.soasta.com), a company that offers CloudTest service. Of course, this is an on-demand cloud service that allows you to use (and pay for) just what you need. SOASTA also offers the free CloudTest Lite product, which you can install on your local computer; It allows to simulate up to 100 simultaneous users. Frankly, since it's free and it's important to design and test a robust application, with a large and fluctuating load, it would be stupid not to use CloudTest Lite.

- Use analytical tools to ensure efficient and effective use of AWS. As you can see from the survey results at the beginning of this chapter, it's easy to use AWS. In fact, it is so easy that you can easily lose track of what you are using or, to be more specific, what you are designing and paying for without buying. Believe me, it's easy to forget all the resources you've put aside. This is not a sign of forgetfulness or neglect; It just happens. The important thing is what you need to do to address this by-product of AWS's easy commission.

Use an analytics tool like Cloudyn (www.cloudyn.com). There are other third-party analytics tools on the market and Amazon has recently launched the new Trusted Advisor service, which is free and allows for some types of similar analysis. Most third-party services also offer a free user level. Given the true cost of unused AWS resources and the availability of free used tools such as Trusted Advisor and other third-party tools, you must use at least one analytics tool to get an idea of your situation. regarding your use of AWS. If the results indicate some gaps in your usage patterns (and probably do, believe us), you can do a deeper analysis by switching to one of the paid options offered by third-party tools, such as Cloudyn.